W9-BKE-238

W9-BKE-238

The Military Jets
Aircraft Guide

The Military Jets Aircraft Guide

Editor: David Donald

CHARTWELL
BOOKS, INC.

Published by
CHARTWELL BOOKS, INC.
A Division of **BOOK SALES, INC.**
114 Northfield Avenue
Edison, New Jersey 08837

Copyright © 1998 Orbis Publishing Ltd
Copyright © 1998 Aerospace Publishing Ltd

Some of this material has previously appeared in the
Orbis reference set 'Airplane'.

All rights reserved. No part of this publication may be reproduced, stored in a retrieval system or
transmitted, in any form or by any means, electronic, mechanical, photocopying, recording or otherwise,
without the prior written permission of the copyright holder.

ISBN: 0-7858-0925-2

Editorial and design by
Brown Packaging Books Ltd
Bradley's Close
74–77 White Lion Street
London N1 9PF

Editor: David Donald

Printed in The Czech Republic

Contents

Messerschmitt Me 262A-1a

Messerschmitt Me 262A-1a fighter in the colours of the 9.Staffel Jagdgeschwader Nr 7, based at Parchim in early 1945 under 1.Jagddivision of I Jagdkorps in the defence of the Reich. After capture at the end of the war this particular aircraft, Nr 500491, was given the code FE-111 by the technical branch of the USAAF for evaluation. In the course of 1979 the aircraft was stripped down, refurbished and rebuilt in over 6,000 hours of work, and placed on display at the National Air and Space Museum, Washington DC, where it remains to this day. The illustration accentuates the Me 262's sleek lines: the airframe alone, in particular the wing design, was considered by the Allies to be far ahead of their own attainments in the field of high-speed flight.

Specification
Messerschmitt Me 262A-1a

Type: single-seat air-superiority fighter

Powerplant: two Junkers Jumo 004B-1, -2, or -3 axial-flow turbojets each rated at 900-kg (1,984-lb) static thrust

Performance: maximum speed 827 km/h (514 mph) at sea level, 852 km/h (530 mph) at 3000 m (9,845 ft), 869 km/h (540 mph) at 6000 m (19,685 ft) and 856 km/h (532 mph) at 8000 m (26,245 ft); initial climb rate 1200 m (3,937 ft) per minute; service ceiling above 12190 m (40,000 ft); range 1050 km (652 miles) at 9000 m (29,530 ft)

Weights: empty 3795 kg (8,378 lb); empty equipped 4413 kg (9,742 lb); maximum take-off 6387 kg (14,080 lb)

Dimensions: span 12.5 m (40 ft 11½ in); length 10.58 m (34 ft 9½ in); height 3.83 m (12 ft 7 in); wing area 21.73 m² (234 sq ft)

Armament: four 30-mm Rheinmetall-Borsig Mk 108A-3 cannon with 100 rounds per gun for the upper pair and 80 rounds per gun for the lower pair, and aimed with Revi 16.B gunsight or EZ.42 gyro-stabilised sight, plus provision for 12 R4M air-to-air rockets under each wing

Keith Fretwell

Gloster Meteor F.Mk 8

Specification
Gloster Meteor F.Mk 8

Type: single-seat interceptor fighter

Powerplant: two 15.5-kN (3,500-lb) thrust Rolls-Royce Derwent 8 turbojets

Performance: maximum speed 953 km/h (592 mph) at sea level, and 885 km/h (550 mph) at 9145 m (30,000 ft); climb to 9180 m (30,000 ft) in 6 minutes 30 seconds; service ceiling 13410 m (44,000 ft); range without wing drop tanks 1111 km (690 miles)

Weights: empty 4846 kg (10,684 lb); maximum take-off 7122 kg (15,700 lb)

Dimensions: span 11.33 m (37 ft 2 in); length 13.59 m (44 ft 7 in); height 3.96 m (13 ft 0 in); wing area 32.515 m² (350.0 sq ft)

Armament: four 20-mm Hispano cannon in the nose with 195 rounds per gun

Possibly one of the most celebrated of all Meteor F.Mk 8s was WF714, the aircraft flown by Squadron Leader Desmond de Villiers, who commanded No. 500 ('County of Kent') Sqn, Royal Auxiliary Air Force, at West Malling, Kent, from September 1952. A de Havilland test pilot by regular profession, de Villiers opted to extend his squadron's chevron markings to the fin and rudder of his Meteor, the blue area (which included the tailplane overall) being symbolic of the Thames estuary and English Channel, the white the chalk cliffs of Dover, and the green the fields of Kent. Despite its auxiliary home defence status, No. 500 Sqn spent its summer camps in Malta and Germany between 1953 and 1956. In common with all auxiliary fighter squadrons, it fell victim to defence cuts and was disbanded in 1957.

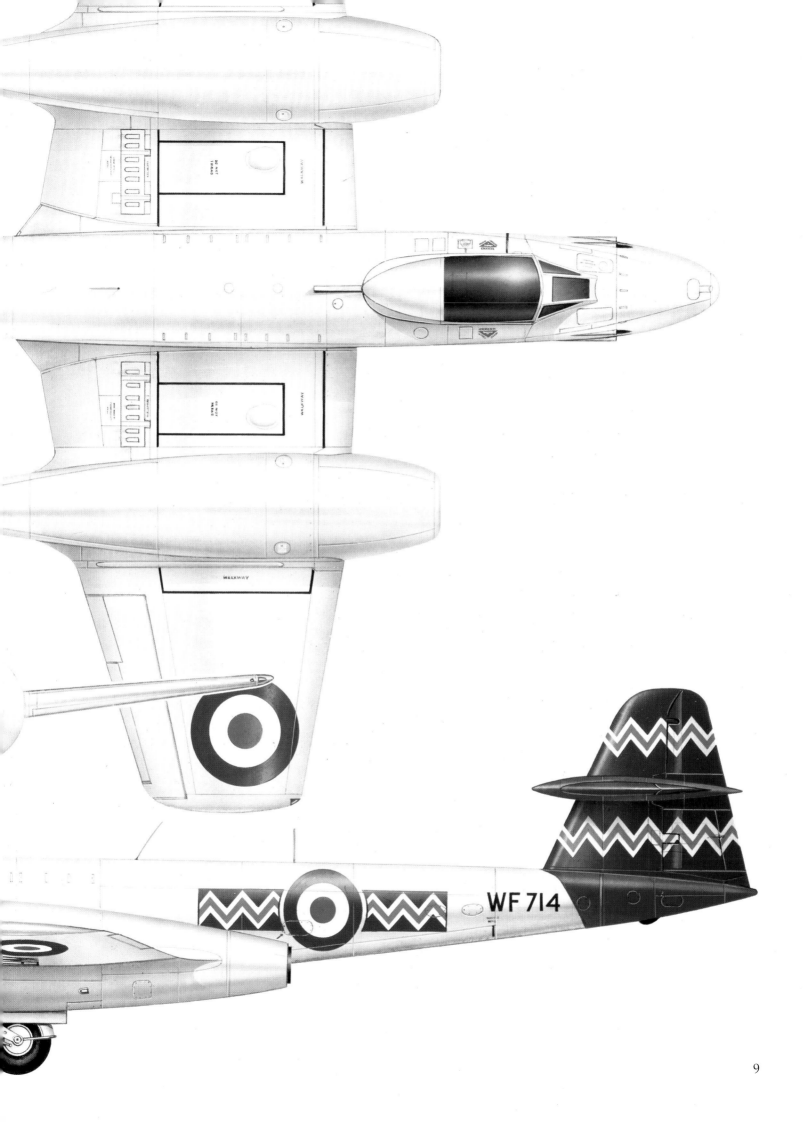

WF 714

Republic F-84F-45-RE

Specification
Republic F-84F-45-RE

Type: single-seat fighter-bomber

Powerplant: one 3275-kg (7,220-lb) thrust Wright J65-W-3 turbojet

Performance: maximum speed 1118 km/h (695 mph) at sea level, 1059 km/h (658 mph) at 6095 m (20,000 ft); initial climb rate 2500 m (8,200 ft) per minute; service ceiling 14020 m (46,000 ft); combat radius (high, with two drop tanks) 1304 km (810 miles)

Weights: empty (typical) 6273 kg (13,830 lb); loaded (clean) 8755 kg (19,340 lb); maximum take-off 12700 kg (28,000 lb)

Dimensions: span 10.24 m (33 ft 7¼ in); length 13.23 m (43 ft 4¾ in); height 4.38 m (14 ft 4¾ in); wing area 30.19 m² (325 sq ft)

Armament: six 12.7-mm (0.5-in) Browning M3 machine-guns; up to 2722 kg (6,000 lb) of external stores originally including US tactical nuclear weapon

U.S. AIR FORCE

Republic F-84 variants

XP-84: three prototypes, last uncompleted, with J35-A-7 engine
YP-84A: pre-production batch of 15 with armament and J35-A-15 engine
F-84B: initial production, Dash-15C engine, ejection seat, some with rocket launchers (total 226)
EF-84B: two F-84B-36-RE modified for tip-tow 'parasite' trials with a B-29 parent aircraft
F-84C: improved systems, Dash-13C engine (total 191)
F-84D: stronger wings, uprated Dash-17D engine (total 154)
F-84E: longer fuselage, inboard bomb/tank pylons, radar ranging sight (total 843)
YF-84F: swept-wing prototype with XJ35-A-25 engine, later given anhedral tailplane and used for FICON trials carried by GRB-36F
F-84F: redesigned production aircraft with J65 engine of various subtypes (total 2,713)
RF-84F: photo-reconnaissance aircraft with longer nose and wing-root inlets (total 715)
GRF-84F: prototype and 25 production aircraft modified for FICON tests carried by GRB-36F; USAF service as **RF-84K**
F-84G: last straight-wing model, J35-A-29 engine, increased bombload, inflight refuelling (total 3,025)
XF-84H: two F-84Fs rebuilt to test supersonic propellers in nose driven by Allison XT40 coupled turboprop, T-tail
YF-84J: two F-84Fs fitted with General Electric J73 engines
F-84KX: F-84B ex-USAF converted for use as US Navy targets (total 80)

Air Force serial 52-6675 identifies this Thunderstreak as an F-84F-45-RE. Like all those manufactured subsequent to Block 25 it has a single-surface 'slab tailplane', and it was illustrated after field modification to fit a braking parachute at the tail of the ventral underfin compartment. The locations of the six guns can be seen in the front elevation, which also highlights the exceptionally wide track which gave excellent ground stability – especially in comparison with the Lockheed F-104. Other points of interest include the spoilers ahead of the flaps, large perforated airbrake on each side of the rear fuselage, and suck-in auxiliary inlet door on each side of the air inlet before it passes under the wing.

de Havilland Vampire variants

D.H.100 (Spidercrab): three prototype aircraft (LZ548/G, LZ551/G and MP838/G); Goblin I engine; first flight 20 September 1943
Vampire Mk I: total of 244 aircraft (including 70 for Sweden and 4 for Switzerland) TG and VF serials; Goblin 2 engine; production by English Electric (TG281, TG283 and TG306 modified as D.H.108; TG283 became VV120); some ex-Swedish aircraft sold to Austria and Dominican Republic
Vampire Mk II: one prototype (TX807) and two Mk I conversions (TG276 and TG280): Nene 1 engine
Vampire F.Mk 3: two prototypes converted from Mk I (TG275 and VF317); production totalled 202 aircraft (including 83 for Canada and 4 for Norway); 15 ex-RAF aircraft to Mexico in 1961; VF, VG, VT and VV serials
Vampire Mk IV: not built as such; project using Nene in Vampire Mk 3 became Vampire Mk 30
Vampire FB.Mk 5: Goblin 2; underwing store provision; 930 for RAF (including 30 later exported to France, 5 to Italy and others to India, Egypt and Venezuela); 41 to Australia, 47 to New Zealand and 17 to South Africa; 67 assembled plus 183 built under licence in France; VV, VX, VZ, WA and WG serials
Vampire FB.Mk 6: Goblin 3 engine; Swiss version, with 75 exported to and 100 licence-built in Switzerland
Vampire Mk 8: Ghost-powered Mk 1 conversion (TG278); one only
Vampire FB.Mk 9: Goblin 3 and tropicalisation modifications; 324 for RAF (including 15 later to Rhodesia and 10 to Jordan), and 2 for Ceylon (but repossessed); WG, WL, WP, WR and WX serials
Vampire Mk 10: two-seater; two prototypes (G-5-2, later WP256, and G-5-5); Goblin 3
Vampire NF.Mk 10: two-seat night-fighter; total of 95 built (62 at Chester, 33 at Hatfield), including 29 (designated **Vampire NF.Mk 54**) for Italy; WM, WP and WV serials
Sea Vampire Mk X: prototype (LZ551) converted for deck trials in 1945
Vampire Mk 11: one prototype (G-5-7); Goblin 3; private-venture two-seat trainer
Vampire T.Mk 11: two-seat trainer; Goblin 35 engine; total of 731 built with WZ, XD, XE, XH and XK serials; 427 built at Chester, remainder at Hatfield; some aircraft assembled by Hindustan Aircraft, India
'Hooked Vampire': three converted Vampire Mk I and Mk 3 (TG328, TG426 and VF315) as prototypes for naval version

Sea Vampire F.Mk 20: 18 aircraft for Fleet Air Arm; VG, VT and VV serials
Sea Vampire Mk 21: three aircraft converted for belly deck-landing trials
Sea Vampire T.Mk 22: 73 aircraft (two-seaters) built for Fleet Air Arm; XA and XG serials
Vampire FB.Mk 25: designation covered 47 Vampire Mk 5s exported to New Zealand (included above)
Vampire F.Mk 30: Australian production; Nene engine; 80 aircraft built
Vampire FB.Mk 31: Australian production; Nene engine; Vampire Mk 5 modification; 29 aircraft built
Vampire F.Mk 32: Australian; one Vampire F.Mk 30 converted with air conditioning
Vampire T.Mk 33: Australian production; Goblin engine; 36 aircraft built
Vampire T.Mk 34: Australian production; five navalised aircraft built
Vampire T.Mk 34A: Australian T.Mk 34s converted to include ejector seats
Vampire T.Mk 35: Australian production; 68 built with increased fuel capacity and revised canopy
Vampire T.Mk 35A: Australian Vampire T.Mk 33s converted to full or partial T.Mk 35 standard
Vampire FB.Mk 50: 143 new-built aircraft exported to Sweden (as **J28**)
Vampire FB.Mk 51: export prototype converted from Vampire Mk 5 (VV658); delivered as pattern aircraft to France
Vampire FB.Mk 52: export version based on Vampire Mk 6; production totalled 101, including 25 for Norway, 50 for Egypt, 6 for Finland, 12 for Iraq and 8 for Lebanon; 7 ex-Egyptian aircraft later went to Jordan
Vampire FB.Mk 52A: 80 aircraft licence-built by Macchi and Fiat in Italy
Vampire FB.Mk 53: 250 aircraft licence-built by SNCASE (France) with Nene engine, and named **Mistral**
Vampire NF.Mk 54: designation covered 29 Vampire Mk 10s (included above) for Italy, then sold to India
Vampire T.Mk 55: 216 new aircraft built for export (Austria 5, Burma 8, Ceylon 5 – repossessed, Chile 5, Egypt 12, Ireland 6, Finland 5, India 55, Indonesia 8, Iraq 6, Lebanon 3, New Zealand 6, Norway 4, Portugal 3, South Africa 21, Sweden 57 as **J28C**, Syria 2 and Venezuela 6); 6 other ex-RAF Vampire T.Mk 11s modified to T.Mk 55 standard for New Zealand, plus 2 to Jordan and 4 to Southern Rhodesia

Specification
de Havilland Vampire FB.Mk 5

Type: single-seat close-support fighter-bomber
Powerplant: one 14-kN (3,100-lb) thrust de Havilland Goblin 2 centrifugal-flow turbojet
Performance: maximum speed 861 km/h (535 mph) at 10365 m (34,000 ft); initial climb rate 1235 m (4,050 ft) per minute; service ceiling 12190 m (40,000 ft); range 1883 km (1,170 miles)
Weights: empty 3290 kg (7,253 lb); maximum take-off 5606 kg (12,360 lb)
Dimensions: span 11.58 m (38 ft 0 in); length 9.37 m (30 ft 9 in); height 2.69 m (8 ft 10 in); wing area 24.34 m^2 (262.0 sq ft)
Armament: gun armament of four 20-mm Hispano cannon in nose, plus an underwing warload of either two 227-kg (500-lb) bombs or eight 27-kg (60-lb) rocket projectiles

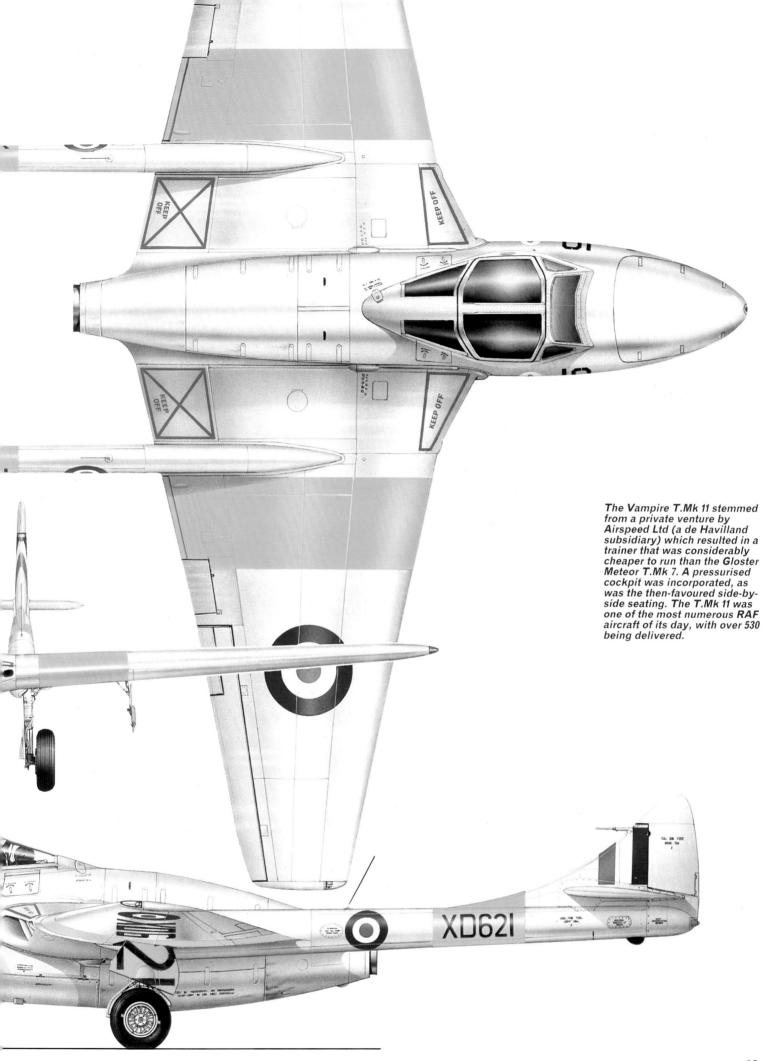

The Vampire **T.Mk 11** stemmed from a private venture by **Airspeed Ltd** (a de Havilland subsidiary) which resulted in a trainer that was considerably cheaper to run than the **Gloster Meteor T.Mk 7**. A pressurised cockpit was incorporated, as was the then-favoured side-by-side seating. The **T.Mk 11** was one of the most numerous **RAF** aircraft of its day, with over 530 being delivered.

XD621

North American F-86F Sabre

'Dottie' was a North American F-86F-30-NA Sabre, serial number 52-4701, flown by Captain D. R. Hall during the Korean War. The aircraft carries the markings of the 336th Fighter Interceptor Squadron of the 4th Fighter Interceptor Wing, based at K-14, the air base at Kimpo, about 40 km (25 miles) north-west of Seoul. The yellow wing and fuselage bands were an ordered identification marking on all F-86s of the Far East Air Forces. The F-86Fs were considerably improved in comparison with the F-86As that had been taking the Korean air war to 'MiG Alley': the later model had more power, increased range capability and a large non-slatted wing enabling the Sabre to turn with the MiG-15.

14

Specification
North American F-86F Sabre
Type: single-seat jet fighter-bomber
Powerplant: one 2682-kg (5,910-lb) thrust General Electric J47-GE-27 turbojet
Performance: maximum speed 1118 km/h (695 mph) at height; initial climb rate (clean) 2835 m (9,300 ft) per minute; service ceiling 14630 m (48,000 ft); range (with drop tanks) 2044 km (1,270 miles)
Weights: empty 4940 kg (10,890 lb); loaded 9234 kg (20,357 lb)
Dimensions: span 11.3 m (37 ft 1 in); length 11.4 m (37 ft 6 in); height 4.4 m (14 ft 8 in); wing area 26.7 m² (288 sq ft)
Armament: six 12.7-mm (0.5-in) machine-guns; provision for two 454-kg (1,000-lb) bombs or many other weapon loads plus two 755-litre (200 US-gal) tanks

U.S. AIR FORCE
24701

FU-701

Mikoyan-Gurevich MiG-15UTI

Specification
Mikoyan-Gurevich MiG-15UTI

Type: two-seat advanced, weapons and conversion trainer

Powerplant: one 26.47-kN (5,952-lb) thrust Klimov VK-1 centrifugal-flow turbojet

Performance: maximum speed 1015 km/h (630 mph) at sea level; service ceiling 15625 m (47,980 ft); range (with either slipper or pylon tanks) 1424 km (885 miles)

Weights: empty 4000 kg (8,820 lb); normal take-off 4850 kg (10,692 lb) clean, 5400 kg (11,905 lb) with guns and drop tanks

Dimensions: wing span 10.08 m (33 ft ¾ in); length 10.04 m (32 ft 11¼ in); height 3.74 m (12 ft 1½ in); wing area 20.6 m² (221.74 sq ft)

Armament: often not fitted; one 23-mm cannon with 80 rounds or one 12.7-mm (0.5-in) machine-gun with 150 rounds; option for two underwing pylons carrying up to 500 kg (1,102 lb) of stores as alternative to drop tanks

Many MiG-15UTI trainers are still in active service around the world, although their numbers are rapidly dwindling. Principal uses for the aircraft are advanced and weapons training, the fact that the aircraft was developed from a successful combat type and that many of its characteristics closely resemble those of later MiG fighters in widespread use making it attractive in these roles. This aircraft wears Iraqi markings, having served (and may still serve) with the training college at Rashid. Even after MiG-15UTIs have been withdrawn from flying status, they have much value as ground instructional airframes.

Identified by its bulbous nose radome, this aircraft is a Canberra T.Mk 17, wearing the Druse Moth insignia of No. 360 Squadron, Royal Air Force. From its base at RAF Wyton, No. 360 Sqn undertakes electronic warfare training missions, supplying jamming to recreate the type of electronic environment that might be experienced in wartime. This gives realistic training for defence systems operators, notably aboard ships of the Royal Navy. The T.Mk 17 is based on the B.Mk 2 airframe, as distinguished at a glance by the short intake centre-bodies. A dozen T.Mk 17s are still on strength with No. 360, most repainted in a tactical 'hemp' scheme and featuring red squadron bars either side of the roundel with yellow lightning flashes.

Specification
BAC Canberra T.Mk 17

Type: high-altitude photo-reconaissance aircraft
Powerplant: two 4990-kg (11,000-lb) thrust Rolls-Royce Avon 206
turbojets
Performance: maximum speed 871 km/h (541 mph) at 12190 m
(40,000 ft); service ceiling 14630 m (48,000 ft); range with maximum
fuel 5842 km (3,630 miles)
Weights: maximum take-off 24925 kg (54,950 lb)
Dimensions: span 9.40 m (30 ft 10 in); length 15.35 m (50 ft 4¼);
height 3.89 m (12 ft 9 in); wing area 49.20 m² (529.60 sq ft)
Armament: one 30-mm ADEN M/55 cannon in starboard wing, two
RB 27 and two RB 28 Falcon missiles, plus up to 1000 kg (2,205 lb) of
bombs or 12 135-mm (5.3-in) Bofors rockets

Keith Fretwell

Hawker Hunter F.Mk 1

Specification
Hawker Hunter F.Mk 1

Type: single-seat interceptor

Powerplant: one 4604-kg (10,150-lb) thrust Rolls-Royce Avon Mk 207 turbojet

Performance: maximum speed 1125 km/h (699 mph) at sea level; service ceiling 15695 m (51,500 ft); combat radius, clean 370 km(230 miles)

Weights: empty 6406 kg (14,122 lb); maximum take-off 10796 kg (23,800 lb)

Dimensions: span 10.25 m (33 ft 8 in); length 13.98 m (45 ft 10½ in); height 4.02 m (13 ft 2 in); wing area 32.42 m² (349 sq ft)

Armament: four 30-mm Aden cannon, plus four underwing pylons carrying 454-kg (1,000-lb) bombs inboard and 227-kg (500-lb) bombs outboard, with provision for up to 24 76-mm (3-in) rocket projectiles, or fuel drop-tanks outboard

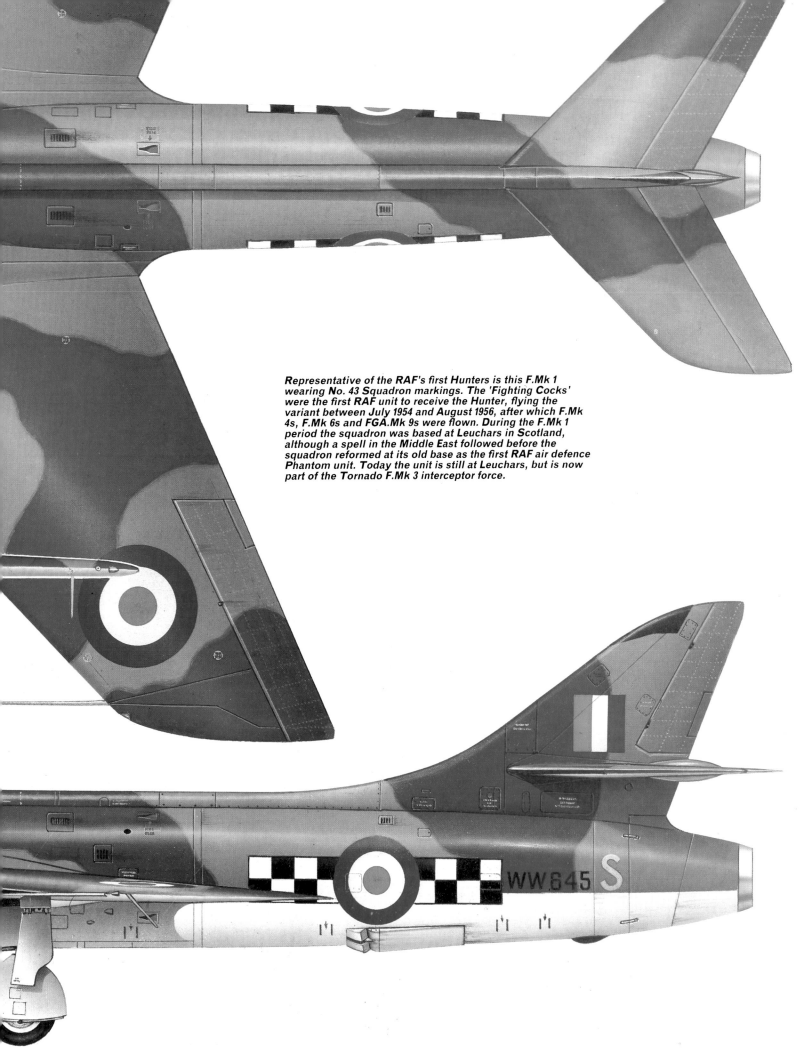

Representative of the RAF's first Hunters is this F.Mk 1 wearing No. 43 Squadron markings. The 'Fighting Cocks' were the first RAF unit to receive the Hunter, flying the variant between July 1954 and August 1956, after which F.Mk 4s, F.Mk 6s and FGA.Mk 9s were flown. During the F.Mk 1 period the squadron was based at Leuchars in Scotland, although a spell in the Middle East followed before the squadron reformed at its old base as the first RAF air defence Phantom unit. Today the unit is still at Leuchars, but is now part of the Tornado F.Mk 3 interceptor force.

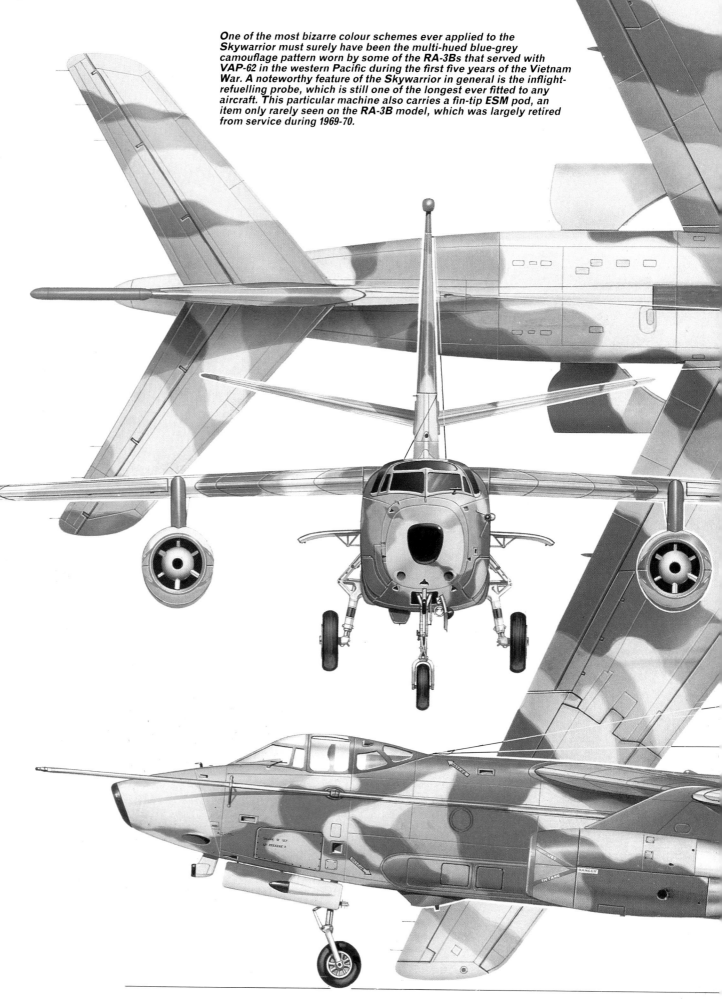

One of the most bizarre colour schemes ever applied to the Skywarrior must surely have been the multi-hued blue-grey camouflage pattern worn by some of the RA-3Bs that served with VAP-62 in the western Pacific during the first five years of the Vietnam War. A noteworthy feature of the Skywarrior in general is the inflight-refuelling probe, which is still one of the longest ever fitted to any aircraft. This particular machine also carries a fin-tip ESM pod, an item only rarely seen on the RA-3B model, which was largely retired from service during 1969-70.

Specification
A-3B Skywarrior

Type: carrierborne bomber aircraft
Powerplant: two Pratt & Whitney J57-P-10 turbojets, each rated at 4763-kg (10,500-lb) dry thrust and 5625-kg (12,400-lb) thrust with water injection
Performance: maximum speed at 3050 m (10,000 ft) 982 km/h (610 mph); service ceiling 12495 m (41,000 ft); tactical radius with standard internal fuel 1690 km (1,050 miles); maximum range 4667 km (2,900 miles)
Weights: empty 17876 kg (39,409 lb); normal loaded 31752 kg (70,000 lb); maximum overload take-off 37195 kg (82,000 lb)
Dimensions: span 22.10 m (72 ft 6 in); length 23.27 m (76 ft 4 in); height 6.95 m (22 ft 9.5 in); wing area 75.43 m^2 (812 sq ft)
Armament: four 907-kg (2,000-lb), or 12 454-kg (1,000-lb) or 24 227-kg (500-lb) bombs housed in internal weapons bay which could also accommodate 'special' (nuclear) weapons; aircraft originally featured twin 20-mm cannon in Westinghouse radar-directed tail barbette, this being deleted in the early 1960s

Keith Fretwell

North American F-100 variants

YF-100A: two prototypes (52-5754/5755) with tall tail and XJ57-P-7 engine
F-100A: initial production day fighter (with unused offensive stores capability), with cut-down vertical tail but original design restored at 71st aircraft and wingspan extended; J57-7 engine; total 203 (52-5766/5778 and 53-1529/1708)
RF-100A: post-1960 rebuild of F-100As as unarmed photo aircraft
YF-100B: redesignated **F-107A,** new design with Y175 engine
F-100C: first fighter-bomber version, eight pylons, FR probe, major systems revision and J57-21 engine; total 476 (451 at Inglewood: 53-1709/1778, 54-1740/2120; and 25 at Columbus: 552709/2733)
TF-100C: redesignated **F-100F**
F-100D: dedicated attack version with full equipment for delivery of increased underwing load including nuclear bombs and Bullpup missiles, modified wing with flaps, revised vertical tail, better avionics and P-21A engine; most stressed for Zell launch; total 1,274 (940 at Inglewood: 54-2121/2303, 55-3502/3814, 56-2903/3346; and 334 at Columbus: 55-2734/2954, 56-3351/3463)
F-100F: tandem dual trainer with reduced armament; total 339, all at Inglewood (56-3725/4019, 58-1205/1233, 58-6975/6983, 59-2558/2563)
DF-100F: conversion as drone (RPV) director
NF-100F: conversions for trials and research
TF-100F: interim Danish F-100F from US stocks

Specification
North American F-100D-75-NA

Type: single-seat fighter-bomber
Powerplant: one Pratt & Whitney J57-P-21A afterburning turbojet with maximum augmenting rating of 7689 kg (16,950 lb)
Performance: maximum speed, clean 1239 km/h (770 mph) or Mach 1.013 at low level, and 1390 km/h (864 mph) or Mach 1.3 at high altitude; initial climb rate, clean 5045 m (16,550 ft) per minute; service ceiling 14020 m (46,000 ft); range at high altitude 966 km (600 miles), or 2492 km (1,500 miles) with two drop tanks
Weights: empty 9526 kg (21,000 lb); clean take-off 13500 kg (29,762 lb); maximum take-off 15800 kg (34,832 lb)
Dimensions: span 11.82 m (38 ft 9½ in); length excluding probe 14.36 m (47 ft 1¼ in); height 4.945 m (16 ft 2⅔ in); wing area 35.77 m² (385.0 sq ft)
Armament: four M39E 20-mm cannon each with 200 rounds, plus up to 3402 kg (7,500 lb) externally carried on eight pylons, including up to six 454-kg (1,000-lb) bombs, four Bullpup air/surface missiles or two AIM-9B Sidewinder AAMs

This illustration shows a North American F-100D-75-NA, company number NA-235-282, USAF serial originally 56-3184 but later prefixed by an O (obsolete) indicating an aircraft over 10 years old. The serial style with black AF63 (actually meaning 1956-63) was introduced in 1968; five years later all numbers were repainted white. On application of camouflage most aircraft lost the red stripes previously used to warn of the potentially dangerous location of the turbine wheels, as well as the black 'buzz number' painted amidships in earlier days. This particular aircraft was assigned to the 416th TFS at Phu Cat AB.

Aermacchi M.B.326H

In its *M.B.326H* form, the *Aermacchi jet was chosen to fill the Royal Australian Air Force's requirement for flying training. The first 12 of the initial batch were built in Italy, but subsequent production was undertaken by Commonwealth Aircraft Corporation at Melbourne, deliveries running from 1967 to 1972. Most wore this attractive yet highly visible orange/white scheme for the training role, but this aircraft also carries underwing machine-gun pods for weapons training. The badge is that of No. 2 Operational Conversion Unit at Williamtown, New South Wales, which conducted conversion training to the Mirage III. Today the unit performs the same task for the F/A-18 Hornet, the Macchis now flying separately as No. 76 Squadron.*

Specification
Aermacchi M.B.326H

Type: two-seat basic/advanced trainer and light attack aircraft

Powerplant: 1547-kg (3,410-lb) static thrust Rolls-Royce Viper 20 Mk 540 in the 326H

Performance: maximum speed 806 km/h (501 mph); range on internal fuel 1665 km (1,035 miles); combat radius 460 km (290 miles); maximum rate of climb at sea level 945 m (3,100 ft) per minute; service ceiling (clean) 12500 m (41,000 ft)

Weights: empty 2237kg (4,930 lb); maximum take-off 3765 kg (8,300 lb); with armament, 5216 kg (11,500 lb)

Dimensions: span over tip-tanks 10.56 m (34 ft 8 in); length 10.65 m (34 ft 11¼ in); height 3.72 m (12 ft 2 in); wing area 19.35 m² (208.3 sq ft)

Armament: two optional 7.7-mm (0.303-in) machine guns in fuselage in early models, with six underwing points for machine-gun pods, rockets and/or bombs, or camera pod(s); maximum external load 907 kg (2,000 lb) on early models, 1814 kg (4,000 lb) on GB and L models

A7-067

Representative of the early Lightning models is this F.Mk 1A, wearing the phoenix badge and red checkerboard of No. 56 Squadron 'Firebrands', based at Wattisham. In its original form, the Lightning had a rounded fin-tip and straight leading edges to the wings. Only a small fuel tank was fitted under the fuselage. Provision was made for a pair of 30-mm ADEN cannon, but the standard armament fit was a pair of de Havilland Firestreak infra-red homing air-to-air missiles mounted on stub pylons either side of the forward fuselage. In the F.Mk 3 and F.Mk 6 the Firestreak could be replaced by the more capable Red Top missile, while Saudi Lightnings could carry ground attack rockets under the forward fuselage and on pylons under the outer wing.

Specification
BAC Lightning F.Mk 1A

Type: single-seat all-weather interceptor, strike and reconaissance aircraft

Powerplant: two 7112-kg (15,680-lb) thrust Rolls-Royce Avon 302 afterburning turbojets

Performance: maximum speed Mach 2.3 or 2415 km/h (1,500 mph) at 12190 m (40,000 ft); range on internal fuel 1287 km (800 miles); initial rate of climb 15240 m (50,000 ft) per min.; time to operational height (around 12190 m/40,000 ft) and speed of Mach 0.92 minutes 30 seconds

Weights: empty equipped about 12700 kg (28,000 lb); maximum take-off 22680 kg (50,000 lb)

Dimensions: span 10.61 m (34 ft 10 in); height 5.97 m (19 ft 7 in); wing area 35.31 m² (380.1 sq ft)

Armament: large, two-portion ventral pack contains fuel tank (rear) and (forward) either more fuel or a pack housing two 30-mm Aden guns (120 rounds each); operational packs mounted ahead of ventral bay include two Firestreak or Red Top air-to-air missiles, or 44 50.4-mm (2-in) spin-stabilised rockets, or five Vinten 360 70-mm cameras, or five Vinten 360 70-mm cameras, or (night reconaissance) cameras and linescan equipment and underwing flares; underwing/overwing hardpoints can carry up to 144 rockets or six 454-kg (1,000-lb) bombs

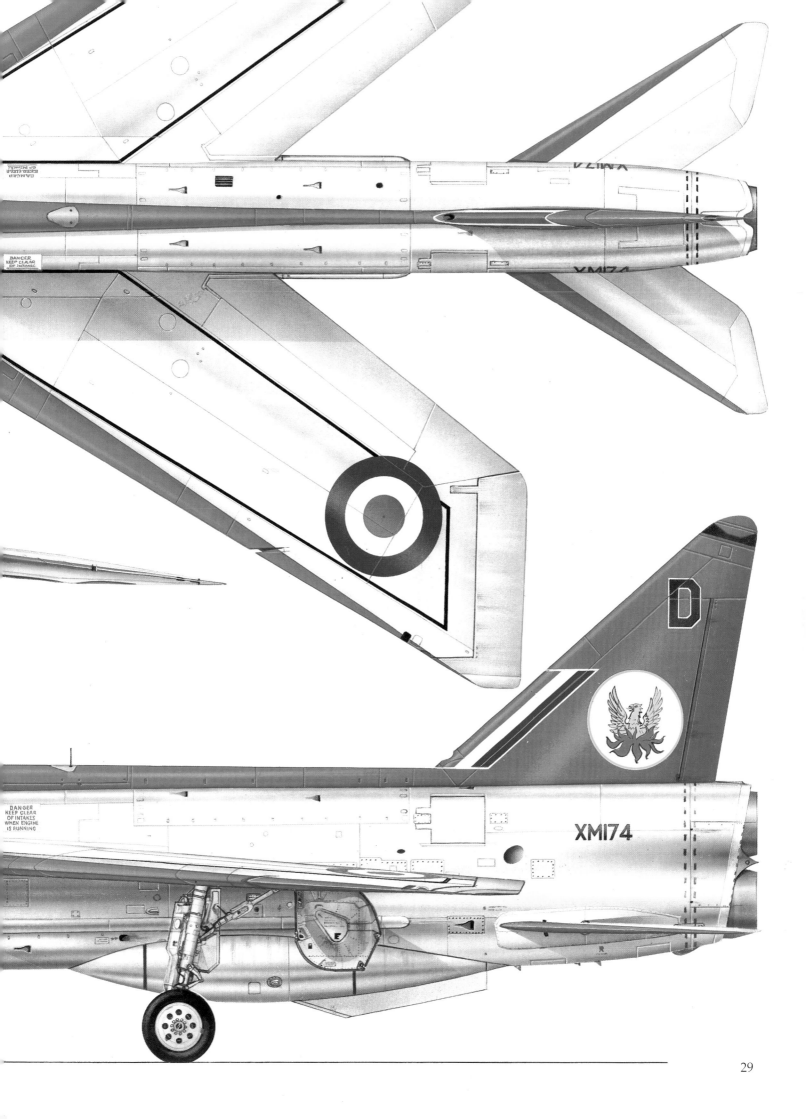

DANGER
KEEP CLEAR
OF INTAKE

DANGER
KEEP CLEAR
OF INTAKE

XM174

DANGER
KEEP CLEAR
OF INTAKES
WHEN ENGINE
IS RUNNING

D

XM174

Douglas F4D-1 Skyray

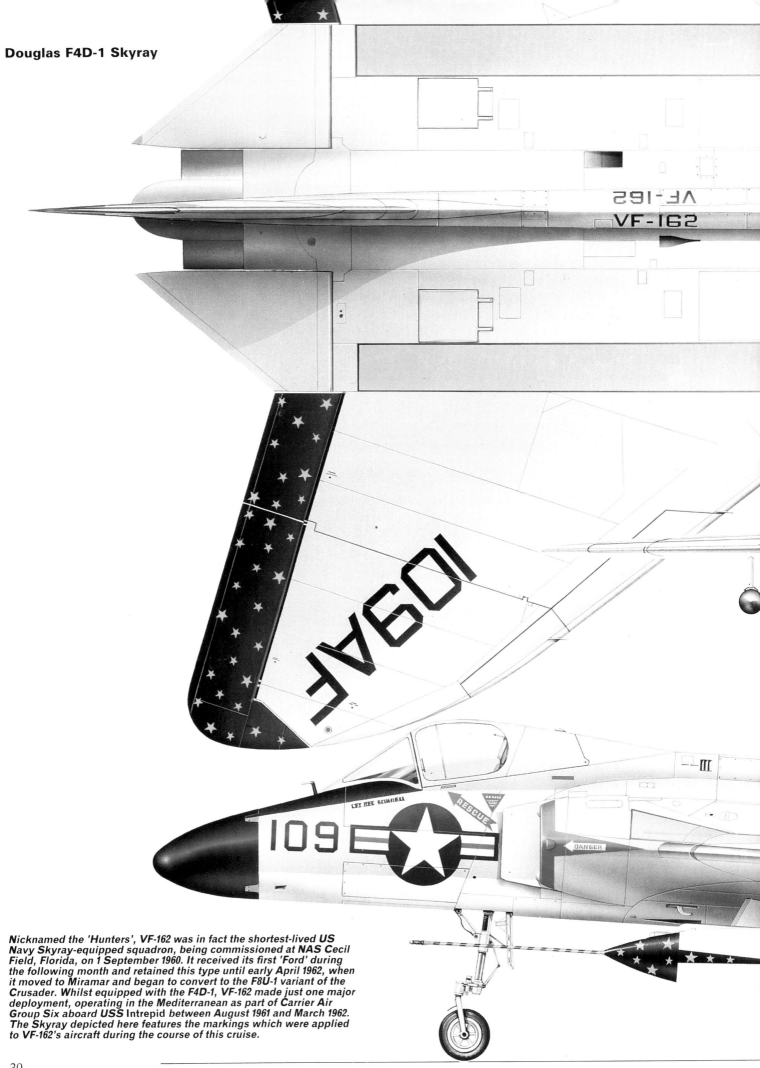

Nicknamed the 'Hunters', VF-162 was in fact the shortest-lived US Navy Skyray-equipped squadron, being commissioned at NAS Cecil Field, Florida, on 1 September 1960. It received its first 'Ford' during the following month and retained this type until early April 1962, when it moved to Miramar and began to convert to the F8U-1 variant of the Crusader. Whilst equipped with the F4D-1, VF-162 made just one major deployment, operating in the Mediterranean as part of Carrier Air Group Six aboard USS Intrepid between August 1961 and March 1962. The Skyray depicted here features the markings which were applied to VF-162's aircraft during the course of this cruise.

XF4D-1: prototype Skyray; two aircraft built
YF4D-1: F4D-1 assigned to development duties; became **YF-6A** in 1962
F4D-1: production version; 419 built for service with US Navy and US Marine Corps; became **F-6A** in 1962
F4D-2: proposal for updated model powered by 4536-kg (10,000-lb) thrust J57-P-14 turbojet engine; project cancelled and none built
F4D-2N: enhanced version of F4D-2 with more capable radar and other improvements; evolved into F5D-1 Skylancer
F5D-1: named **Skylancer**; improved Skyray with J57-P-12 engine, enlarged tail surfaces, lengthened nose and thinner wing aerofoil; two prototypes and two development specimens built and flown, but plans for production abandoned in favour of F-8U Crusader.

Specification
Douglas F4D-1 Skyray

Type: single-seat all-weather interceptor fighter

Powerplant: one Pratt & Whitney J57-P-8A turbojet rated at 4627-kg (10,200-lb) dry and 7258-kg (16,000-lb) afterburning thrust

Performance: maximum speed at sea level 1162 km/h (722 mph); maximum speed at 10973 m (36,000 ft) 1118 km/h (695 mph); cruising speed 837 km/h (520 mph); initial climb rate 5578 m (18,300 ft) per minute; service ceiling 16764 m (55,000 ft); normal range 1127 km (700 miles); maximum range 1931 km (1,200 miles)

Weights: empty 7268 kg (16,024 lb); normal loaded 9983 kg (22,008 lb); maximum take-off 12300 kg (27,116 lb)

Dimensions: span 10.21 m (33 ft 6 in); length 13.79 m (45 ft 3 in); height 3.96 m (13 ft 0 in); wing area 51.75 m^2 (557 sq ft)

Armament: four integral 20-mm cannon, plus up to 1814 kg (4,000 lb) of bombs, rocket pods, AIM-9 Sidewinder air-to-air missiles or auxiliary fuel tanks mounted on seven external hardpoints

VF-162

09

AF
4957
NAVY

Keith Fretwell

31

McDonnell RF-101C Voodoo

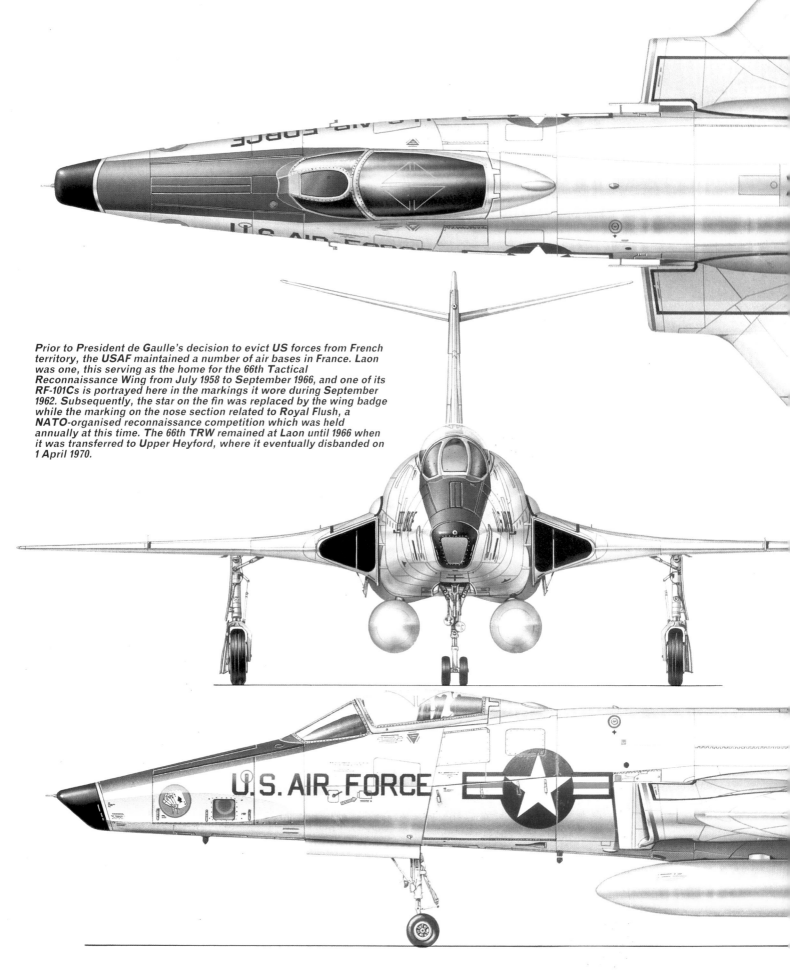

Prior to President de Gaulle's decision to evict US forces from French territory, the USAF maintained a number of air bases in France. Laon was one, this serving as the home for the 66th Tactical Reconnaissance Wing from July 1958 to September 1966, and one of its RF-101Cs is portrayed here in the markings it wore during September 1962. Subsequently, the star on the fin was replaced by the wing badge while the marking on the nose section related to Royal Flush, a NATO-organised reconnaissance competition which was held annually at this time. The 66th TRW remained at Laon until 1966 when it was transferred to Upper Heyford, where it eventually disbanded on 1 April 1970.

Specification
McDonnell RF-101C Voodoo

Type: single-seat tactical reconnaissance aircraft

Powerplant: two Pratt & Whitney J57-13 turbojets each rated at 66.2 kN (14,880 lb) with maximum afterburner

Performance: maximum speed (clean, at height) Mach 1.7 (1802 km/h; 1.120 mph); service ceiling 15850 m (52,000 ft); range (with internal fuel at high altitude) 3040 km (1,890 miles), (with two 1705-litre/375-gal drop tanks) 3862 km (2,400 miles)

Weights: empty, equipped 11617 kg (25,610 lb); loaded (clean) 19300 kg (42,550 lb); maximum (with two tanks) 22099 kg (48,720 lb)

Dimensions: span 12.09 m (39 ft 8 in); length 21.1 m (69 ft 3 in); height 5.49 m (18 ft 0 in); wing area 34.19 m^2 (368 sq ft)

Armament: none

Keith Fretwell.

Specification
Shenyang J-6

Type: single-seat day fighter-bomber

Powerplant: two 32.36-kN (7,275-lb) thrust Tumanskii RD-9BM afterburning turbojets

Performance: maximum speed 1452 km/h (902 mph) at height; initial climb 6900 m (22,635 ft) per minute; absolute ceiling 19870 m (65,190 ft); combat radius with two 800-litre (176-Imp gal) underwing tanks 685 km (426 miles); ferry range 2200 km (1,366 miles)

Weights: empty 5760 kg (12,700 lb); maximum take-off 8700 kg (19,180 lb)

Dimensions: span 9.20 m (30 ft 2¼ in); length (excluding nose probe) 12.60 m (41 ft 4 in); height 3.88 m (12 ft 8¾ in); wing area 25.00 m² (269 sq ft)

Armament: two or three 30-mm NR-30 cannon each with 73 rounds; provision for two bombs of up to 454-kg (1,000-lb) size (usually half this size), various single- or multi-barrelled pod rockets or four AIM-9B Sidewinder AAMs

This J-6 is one of at least two painted in this lurid red/yellow colour scheme in service with Pakistan air force's No. 25 Squadron at Sargodha, which is one of three operational conversion units equipped with the J-6 and two-seat FT-6. Though it is unlikely that more modern engines will ever be fitted (the Rolls-Royce/Turboméca Adour has been considered) the Pakistani J-6 squadrons are having their aircraft progressively updated. One of the first significant changes was the braking parachute compartment below the rudder; others include fitting Martin-Baker PKD.10 seats, wiring and racks for Sidewinder AAMs, newer instruments and a ventral centreline drop tank.

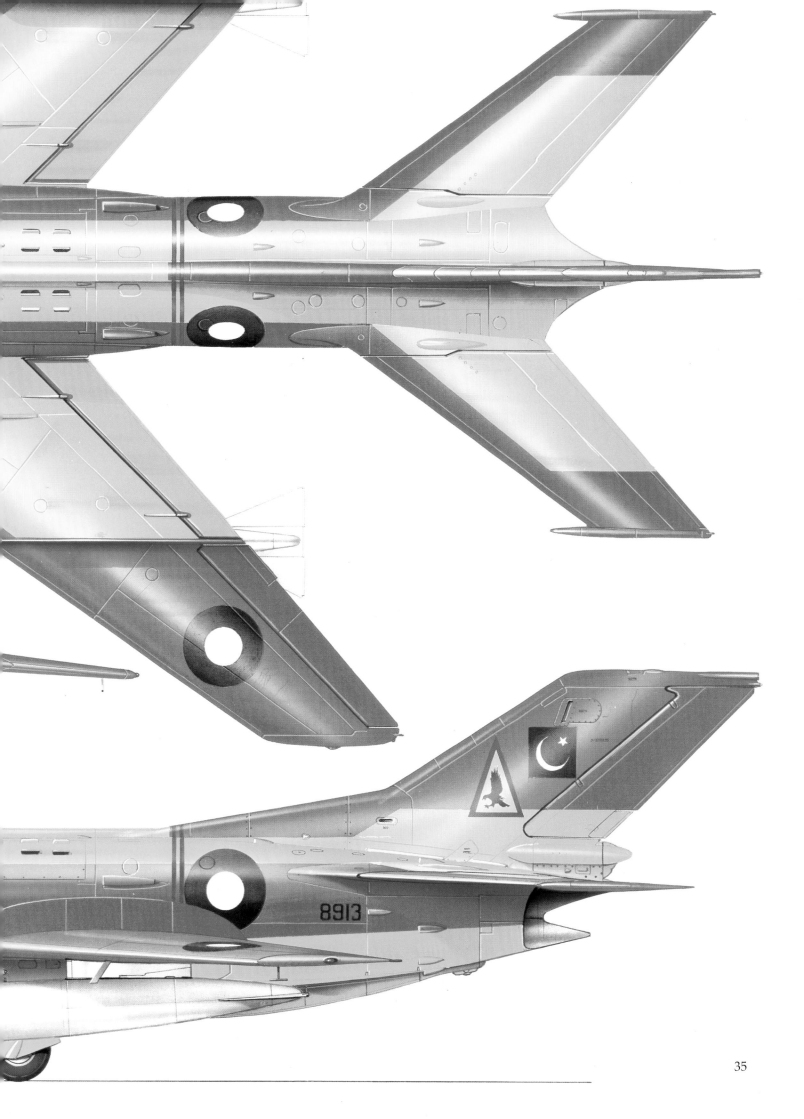

8913

Vought F-8E Crusader

Specification
Vought F-8E Crusader

Type: single-seat naval fighter

Powerplant: one 8165-kg (18,000-lb) Pratt & Whitney J57-P-20A afterburning turbojet

Performance: maximum speed (clean) 1800 km/h (1,120 mph), Mach 1.7 at 12192 m (40,000 ft); climbs to 17374 m (57,000 ft) in six minutes; service ceiling 17983 m (59,000 ft); radius at high altitude 966 km (600 miles)

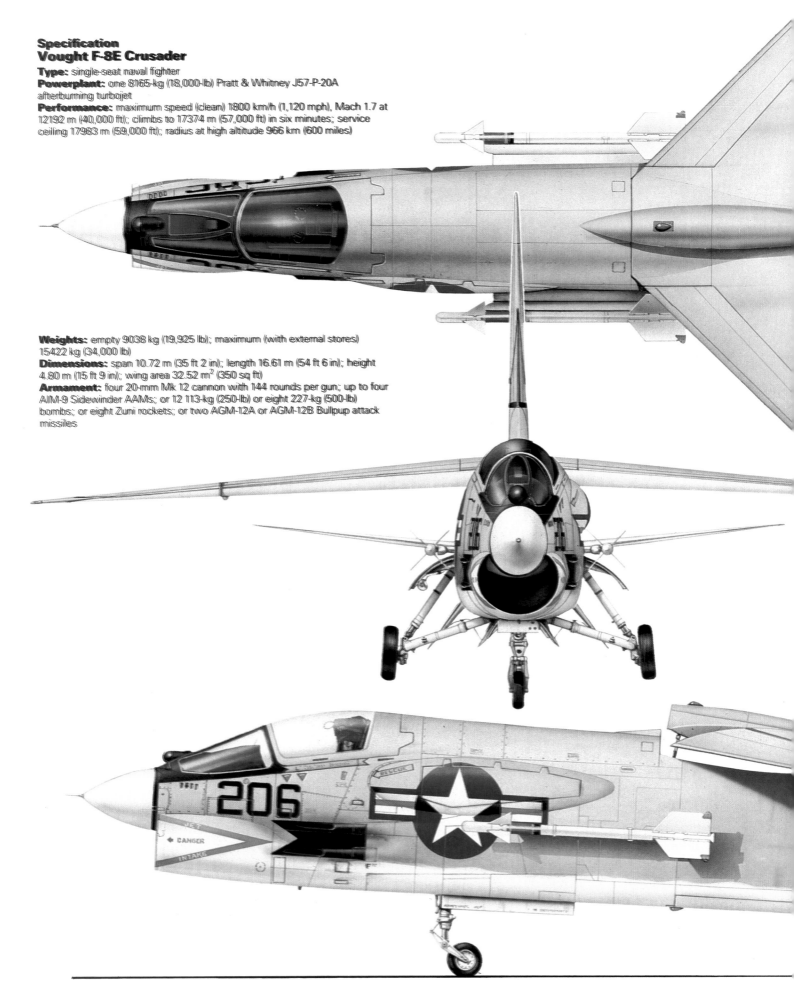

Weights: empty 9038 kg (19,925 lb); maximum (with external stores) 15422 kg (34,000 lb)

Dimensions: span 10.72 m (35 ft 2 in); length 16.61 m (54 ft 6 in); height 4.80 m (15 ft 9 in); wing area 32.52 m² (350 sq ft)

Armament: four 20-mm Mk 12 cannon with 144 rounds per gun; up to four AIM-9 Sidewinder AAMs; or 12 113-kg (250-lb) or eight 227-kg (500-lb) bombs; or eight Zuni rockets; or two AGM-12A or AGM-12B Bullpup attack missiles

US Navy involvement in the Vietnam War gave the Crusader the chance to prove its worth in deadly combat, a challenge to which it responded magnificently. No less than 17 MiG-17s were downed by its Sidewinder AAMs; supersonic MiG-21s were also destroyed, and the Crusader's 20-mm forward-mounted cannon also scored victories in the air. The relatively small and light design enabled the Crusader to operate from the smaller carriers, in this instance an F-8E from USS Hancock (CVA-19) during March 1967.

This illustration shows a standard **B-58A** of **USAF**'s **Strategic Air Command**. It was normal to display the Command's star-spangled fuselage band and badge, but not unit insignia. This aircraft, however, is believed to have served with the 305th Bombardment Wing (Medium) at Peru (later Grissom) AFB, Indiana. What cannot be brought out fully is the characteristic nose-down sit of the B-58 on the ground, but visible are the roof hatches for entry and exit of the three crew-members, the tail 'Gatling gun' mounted like the sting of a wasp and trainable over an arc at the rear, the enormous payload pod which conformed with the supersonic area rule when in place, the rectangular landing-gear boxes which projected above and below the wing, and the gateleg nose gear which contrived to avoid the nose of the pod.

Specification
General Dynamics Convair B-58A
Type: three-seat supersonic bomber
Powerplant: four General Electric J79-5B augmented turbojets, each rated at 69.4 kN (15,600 lb) with maximum afterburner
Performance: maximum speed at sea level 1128 km/h (701 mph), and at high altitude 2128 km/h (1,322 mph); range 8248 km (5,125 miles) without refuelling
Weights: empty without pod 25202 kg (55,560 lb); maximum take-off 73937 kg (163,000 lb); after inflight refuelling 80342 kg (177,120 lb)
Dimensions: span 17.32 m (56 ft 10 in); length 29.49 m (96 ft 9 in); height 9.58 m (31 ft 5 in); wing area 143.35 m² (1,543 sq ft)
Armament: maximum drop weight 8823 kg (19,450 lb) including pod(s), with any six types of nuclear bomb including B43 and B61; one 20-mm T-171 tail gun

Convair F-106A Delta Dart

The Convair F-106A Delta Dart became one of the classic shapes of post-war military aviation, its needle nose and delta wing signifying both speed and manoeuvrability. In 1960s terms its performance matched its looks, but by the 1980s the 'Six' was being overshadowed by greater numbers of more modern types. This aircraft is representative of the last F-106s in service, which soldiered on with Air National Guard units into the late 1980s, when most were replaced in the US defence role by General Dynamics F-16s. It wears the markings of the 159th Fighter Interceptor Squadron, Florida Air National Guard.

Specification
Convair F-106A Delta Dart

Type: single-seat supersonic all-weather interceptor

Powerplant: one 11113-kg (24,500-lb) afterburning thrust Pratt & Whitney J75-P-17 turbojet

Performance: maximum speed 2454 km/h (1,525 mph) or Mach 2.31 at 12190 m (40,000 ft); service ceiling 17375 m (57,000 ft); combat radius with external fuel tanks 1173 km (729 miles)

Weights: empty 10728 kg (23,646 lb); maximum take-off for area interceptor mission 17554 kg (38,700 lb); maximum take-off 18975 kg (41,831 lb)

Dimensions: span 11.67 m (38 ft 3½ in); length 21.56 m (70 ft 8¾ in); height 6.18 m (20 ft 3¼ in); wing area 58.65 m² (631.3 sq ft)

Armament: one Douglas AIR-2A Genie or AIR-2B Super Genie rocket, and four Hughes AIM-4F or AIM-4G Super Falcon air-to-air missiles carried in internal weapons bay; many aircraft also have one 20-mm M61 Vulcan gun in place of Genie

Keith Fretwell

F-102A Delta Dagger

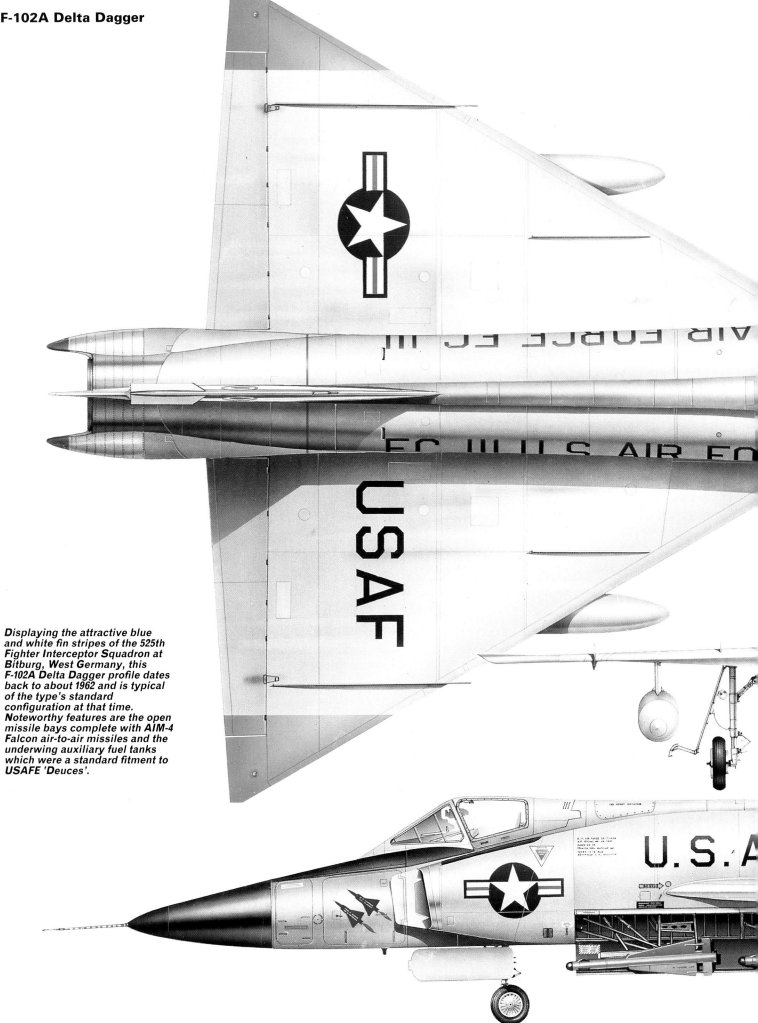

Displaying the attractive blue and white fin stripes of the 525th Fighter Interceptor Squadron at Bitburg, West Germany, this F-102A Delta Dagger profile dates back to about 1962 and is typical of the type's standard configuration at that time. Noteworthy features are the open missile bays complete with AIM-4 Falcon air-to-air missiles and the underwing auxiliary fuel tanks which were a standard fitment to USAFE 'Deuces'.

Specification
Convair F-102A Delta Dagger

Type: single-seater interceptor

Powerplant: one Pratt & Whitney J57-P-23 turbojet rated at 52 kN (11,700 lb) dry and 77 kN (17,200 lb) afterburning thrust

Performance: maximum speed, clean at 12190 m (40,000 ft) 1328 km/h (825 mph); normal cruise speed at 10670 m (35,000 ft) 869 km/h (540 mph); initial climb rate 5304 m (17,400 ft) per minute; service ceiling 16460 m (54,000 ft); tactical radius with two 871-litre (230-US gal) drop tanks and full armament 805 km (500 miles) at 869 km/h (540 mph); maximum range 2173 km (1,350 miles)

Weights: normal loaded, clean 12565 kg (27,700 lb); normal loaded, point interceptor 12769 kg (28,150 lb); maximum take-off 14288 kg (31,500 lb)

Dimensions: span 11.62 m (38 ft 1.5 in); length 20.84 m (68 ft 4.6 in); height 6.46 m (21 ft 2.5 in); wing area 61.45 m^2 (661.5 sq ft)

Armament: three AIM-4C Falcon infra-red homing air-to-air missiles and one AIM-26A Nuclear Falcon, or three AIM-4A/4E beam-riding and three AIM-4C/4F infra-red homing air-to-air missiles; up to 24 unguided 70-mm (2.75-in) folding-fin aerial rockets were originally carried but these were eventually deleted

Keith Fretwell.

Avro Canada CF-105 Arrow

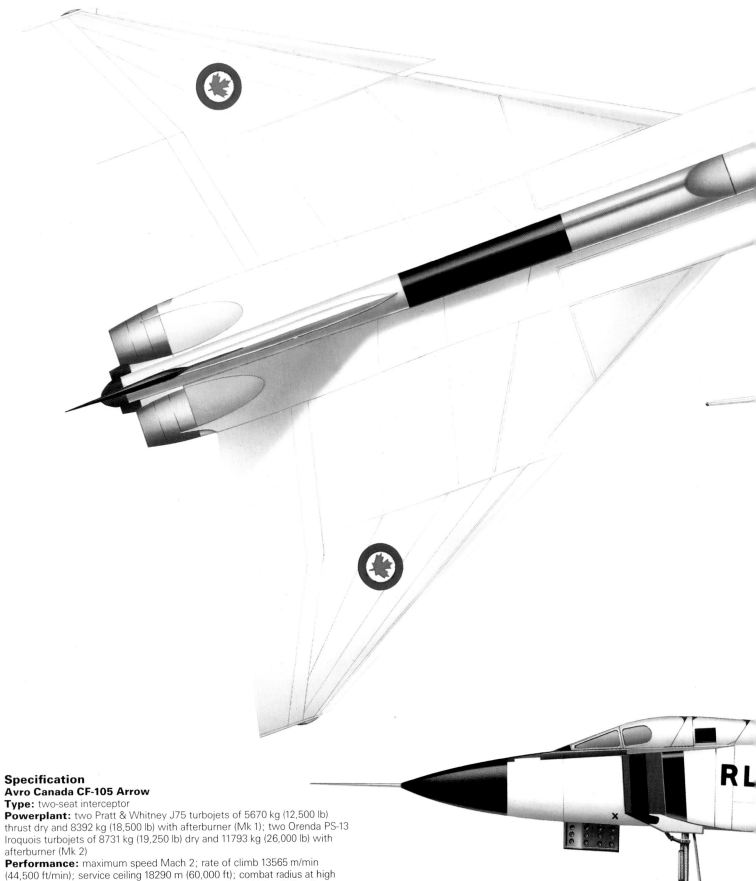

Specification
Avro Canada CF-105 Arrow
Type: two-seat interceptor
Powerplant: two Pratt & Whitney J75 turbojets of 5670 kg (12,500 lb) thrust dry and 8392 kg (18,500 lb) with afterburner (Mk 1); two Orenda PS-13 Iroquois turbojets of 8731 kg (19,250 lb) dry and 11793 kg (26,000 lb) with afterburner (Mk 2)
Performance: maximum speed Mach 2; rate of climb 13565 m/min (44,500 ft/min); service ceiling 18290 m (60,000 ft); combat radius at high speed 483 km (300 miles); maximum combat radius 660 km (410 miles)
Weights: empty 22244 kg (49,000 lb) (Mk 1); maximum overload 31117 kg (68,500 lb) (Mk 1), 31228 kg (69,000 lb) (Mk 2)
Dimensions: wing span 15.24 m (50 ft); length 25.3 m (83 ft) (Mk 1), 24.38 m (80 ft) (Mk 2); height 6.25 m (20 ft 6 in) (Mk 1), 6.4 m (21 ft) (Mk 2); wing area 113.8 m² (1,225 sq ft)
Armament: none (Mk 1); six Falcon air-to-air missiles (Mk 2)

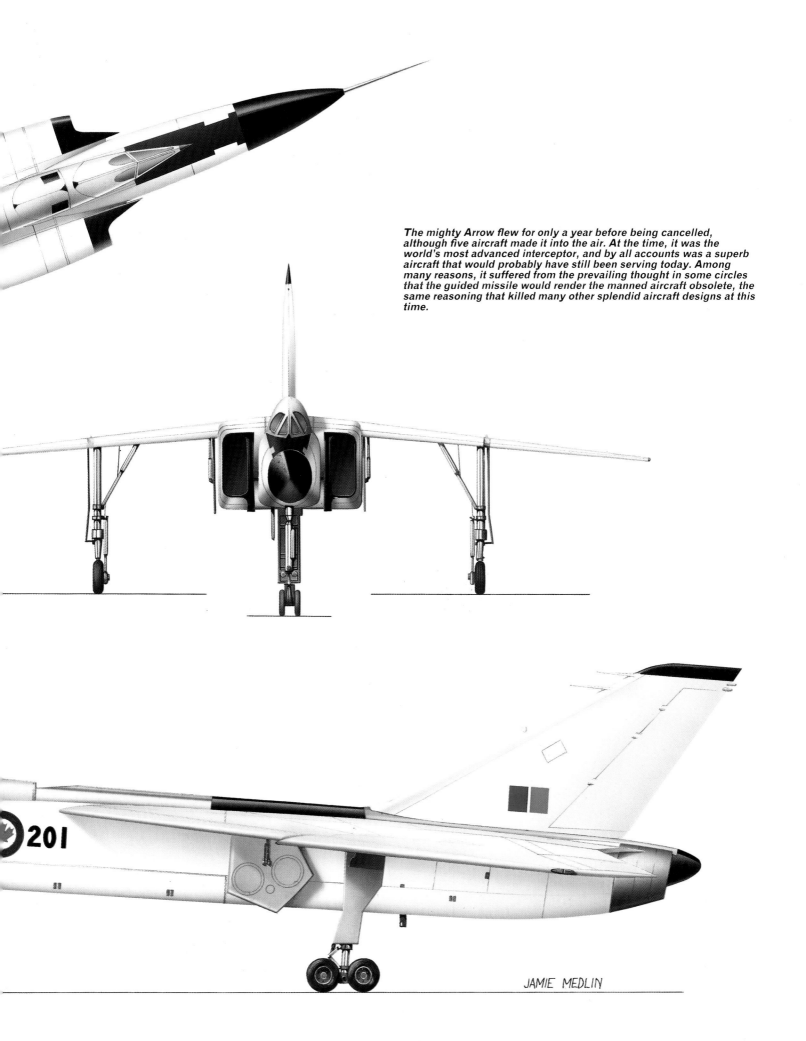

The mighty Arrow flew for only a year before being cancelled, although five aircraft made it into the air. At the time, it was the world's most advanced interceptor, and by all accounts was a superb aircraft that would probably have still been serving today. Among many reasons, it suffered from the prevailing thought in some circles that the guided missile would render the manned aircraft obsolete, the same reasoning that killed many other splendid aircraft designs at this time.

201

JAMIE MEDLIN

Specification
Blackburn B-103 Buccaneer

Type: two-seat carrier- or land-based low-level strike aircraft

Powerplant: two 5105-kg (11,255-lb) thrust Rolls-Royce RB.168 Spey Mk101 turbofans

Performance: maximum speed 1040 km/h (646 mph) at 61 m (200 ft); service ceiling over 12190 m (40,000 ft); typical range with weapons 3701 km (2,300 miles)

Weights: empty 13608 kg (30,000 lb); maximum take-off 28123 kg (62,000 lb)

Dimensions: span 13.41 m (44 ft 0 in); length 19.33 m (63 ft 5 in); height 4.97 m (16 ft 3 in); wing area 47.82m² (514.7 sq ft)

Armament: four 454-kg (1,000-lb) bombs, fuel tank, or reconaissance pack on inside of rotary bomb door, and up to 5443 kg (12,000 lb) of bombs and/or missiles on four underwing hardpoints

XZ430 was from the last batch of Buccaneers, delivered to the RAF in 1977. Features of the last production configuration were the bulged bomb bay housing additional fuel and the fin-mounted radar warning receivers. The aircraft serves with No. 208 Squadron at RAF Lossiemouth, where it partners No. 12 Squadron in the anti-shipping role, employing the Sea Eagle and Martel missile. A secondary role is providing laser designation for the Tornado GR.Mk 1 force. The area-ruling of the fuselage gives the 'Bucc' its distinctive shape, right down to the extended bulged tailcone, which doubles as a split airbrake.

XZ430

Keith Fretwell

A *S*aab *D*raken in the markings of
*F*10 wing of the *S*wedish air force,
based at *Å*ngelhom in the *S*outh
*S*weden military command. The *J*
35F, or 'Filip', was *S*aab's first
attempt at a fully integrated
weapons system, an approach
later much refined with the *V*iggen.
This *D*raken differs from earlier
versions in having a more powerful
*E*ricsson *PS*-01 radar, *S*aab *S7B*
collision-course fire control and
FH5 autopilot. It also introduced a
zero-zero ejection seat and a
single-piece blown hood. The left-
hand cannon was deleted to
provide extra avionics space.

Specification
SAAB-35 Draken

Type: single-seat interceptor

Powerplant: one 7830-kg (17,262-lb) afterburning thrust Flygmotor RM6C (licence-built) Rolls Royce Avon 300 turbojet

Performance: maximum speed, clean Mach 2 or 2125 km/h (1,320 mph) at 11000 m (36,090 ft); service ceiling 20000 m (65,615 ft); hi-lo-hi radius on internal fuel 560 km (348 miles)

Weights: empty 7425 kg (16,369 lb); maximum take-off 12700 kg (27,998 lb)

Dimensions: span 9.40 m (30 ft 10 in); length 15.35 m (50 ft 4¾ in); height 3.89 m (12 ft 9 in); wing area 49.20 m² (529.60 sq ft)

Armament: one 30-mm ADEN M/55 cannon in starboard wing, two RB 27 and two RB 28 Falcon missiles, plus up to 1000 kg (2,205 lb) of bombs or 12 135-mm (5.3-in) Bofors rockets

Keith Fretwell.

49

Mikoyan-Gurevich MiG-21bis 'Fishbed-N'

Typical of many late-model MiG-21s still in Soviet service, this is a MiG-21bis 'Fishbed-N'. The MiG-21bis introduced the uprated Tumanskii R-25-300 jet, rated at 73.6 kN (16,535 lb) thrust, the late 'Fishbed-N' version offering further improvements to avionics, as indicated by the 'Swift Rod' ILS antennae under the nose and on the fin. This aircraft is carrying a standard air-to-air load of four 'Atoll' air-to-air missiles. On the inboard pylons are AA-2D infra-red guided missiles, while the weapons outboard are AA-2C semi-active radar-guided missiles. The MiG-21bis also routinely carries the far more capable AA-8 'Aphid' in place of the AA-2Ds.

Specification
Mikoyan-Gurevich MiG-21bis 'Fishbed-N'
Type: single-seat multi-role fighter
Powerplant: one Tumanskii R-25 turbojet with afterburning
thrust of 73.5-kN (16,535 lb)
Performance: maximum speed 2230 km/h (1,386 mph) or
Mach 2.1 above 11000 m (36,090 ft); service ceiling 15250 m
(50,035 ft); maximum range with internal fuel 11000 km (684
miles)
Weights: maximum take-off 9400 kg (20,723 lb)
Dimensions: span 7.15 m (23 ft 5½ in); length 15.76 m
(51 ft 8½ in); height 410 m (13 ft 5½ in); wing area 23 m²
(247.58 sq ft)
Armament: one 23-mm Gsh-23 twin-barrel cannon in
underbelly pack, plus about 1500 kg (3,307 lb) of stores on
four underwing pylons

Specification
Republic F-105D Thunderchief

Type: single-seat strike fighter

Powerplant: one Pratt & Whitney J75-P-19W turbojet rated at 7802 kg (17,200 lb) thrust dry and 11113 kg (24,500 lb) thrust with afterburning; water injection permits 60-second rating of 12020 kg (26,500 lb) thrust in afterburner mode

Performance: maximum speed 2,237 km/h (1,390 mph) or Mach 2.1 at 10970 m (36,000 ft); initial climb rate 10485 m (34,400 ft) per minute in clean configuration; service ceiling 12560 m (41,200 ft) on a typical mission; range 1480 km (920 miles) with two 1703-litre (450-US gal) drop-tanks underwing, one 2461-litre (650-US gal) drop-tank on centreline and two AGM-12 Bullpup ASMs; ferry range 3846 km (2,390 miles) with maximum external fuel at 940 km/h (584 mph)

Weights: empty 12,474 kg (27,500 lb); maximum overload take-off 23967 kg (52,838 lb)

Dimensions: span 10.59 m (34 ft 9 in); length 19.61 m (64 ft 4 in); height 5.97 m (19 ft 7 in); wing area 35.77 m^2 (385.0 sq ft)

Armament: combinations of 340-kg (750-lb) M117 bombs, 454-kg (1,000-lb) Mk 83 bombs, 1361-kg (3,000-lb) M118 bombs, AGM-12 Bullpup ASMs, AIM-9 Sidewinder AAMs, 70-mm (2.75-in) rocket pods, napalm containers, Mk 28/43 special weapons, chemical bombs, leaflet bombs, 127-mm (5-in) rocket pods and MLU-10/B mines; also one M61 Vulcan 20-mm cannon with 1,028 rounds of ammunition

YF-105A: two prototypes each powered by Pratt & Whitney J57-P-25 engines rated at 6804-kg (15,000-lb) thrust

F-105B: initial production model; total of 75 built, including 10 for RDT & E purposes; powered by Pratt & Whitney J57-P-3 rated at 7484-kg (16,500-lb) thrust

RF-105B: proposed reconnaissance model; three prototypes ordered but completed as JF-105B RDT & E aircraft when reconnaissance variant abandoned

JF-105B: three aircraft built for systems test work using those airframes originally laid down as RF-105B prototypes

F-105C: projected tandem two-seat operational trainer derivative of F-105B; subsequently abandoned after reaching mock-up stage

F-105D: definitive single-seat Thunderchief model, 610 being built; powered by Pratt & Whitney J75-P-19W rated at 7802 kg (17,200 lb) thrust

RF-105D: proposed reconnaissance variant of F-105D; abandoned in December 1961 in favour of RF-4C Phantom

F-105E: projected tandem two-seat operational trainer variant of F-105D; construction begun but abandoned, those aircraft on assembly line being completed as F-105Ds

F-105F: two-seat combat proficiency trainer varaint based on F-105D; 143 built

EF-105F: initial designation applied to 'Wild Weasel' SAM suppression model which ultimately became the F-105G

F-105G: ultimate 'Wild Weasel' SAM suppression aircraft, approximately 60 F-105Fs being converted to this configuration

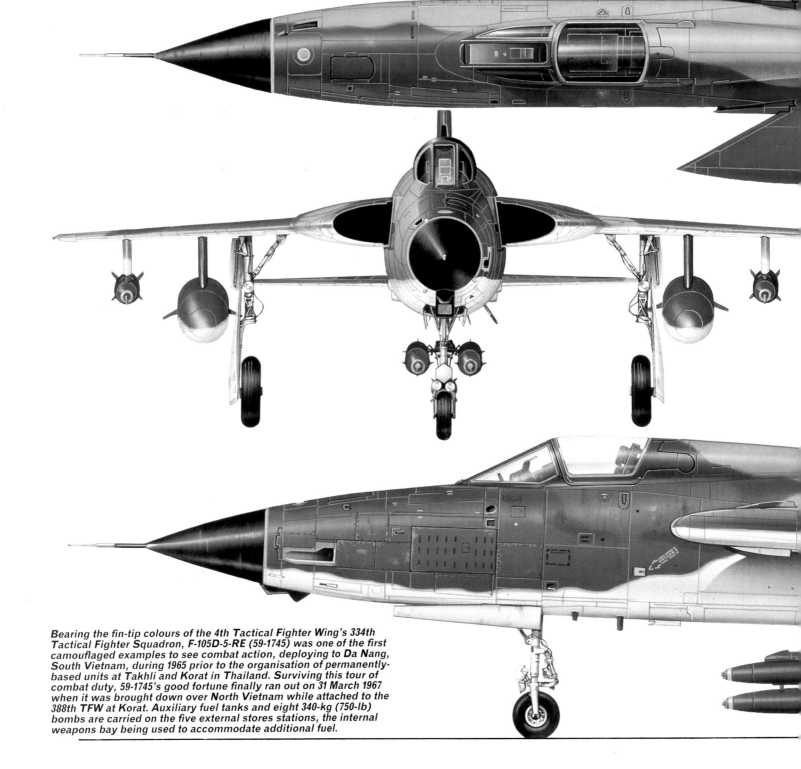

Bearing the fin-tip colours of the 4th Tactical Fighter Wing's 334th Tactical Fighter Squadron, F-105D-5-RE (59-1745) was one of the first camouflaged examples to see combat action, deploying to Da Nang, South Vietnam, during 1965 prior to the organisation of permanently-based units at Takhli and Korat in Thailand. Surviving this tour of combat duty, 59-1745's good fortune finally ran out on 31 March 1967 when it was brought down over North Vietnam while attached to the 388th TFW at Korat. Auxiliary fuel tanks and eight 340-kg (750-lb) bombs are carried on the five external stores stations, the internal weapons bay being used to accommodate additional fuel.

Republic F-105D Thunderchief

USAF
91745

Keith Fretwell.

Lockheed F-104G Starfighter

The Starfighter is best-known wearing the iron cross of West Germany. Huge numbers served with both the Luftwaffe and the Marineflieger, although they have now been replaced by Tornados. In West German service the 'Star' developed a reputation for a high attrition rate, drawing the epithet 'Widowmaker' from the popular press. In fact the type was highly regarded by its pilots, many of whom mourned its passing when they had to convert to the two-seat Tornado. Its attrition rate, while high by today's standards, was nevertheless considerably lower than many other contemporary aircraft, and it was lower than for many other Starfighter operators. This aircraft is one of the F-104Gs supplied to the German navy, wearing the badge of Marinefliegergeschwader 1 based at Schleswig. It is seen armed with MBB Kormoran anti-ship missiles on the wing pylons, and with practice bombs on the centreline. In addition to the anti-ship F-104Gs, the Marineflieger also had RF-104G tactical reconnaissance aircraft, these serving with MFG 2 and making daily flights along the Baltic coasts of East Germany and Poland.

Specification
Lockheed F-104G Starfighter

Type: single-seat multi-mission fighter

Powerplant: one General Electric J79-GE-11A turbojet of 7076 kg (15,600 lb) afterburning thrust

Performance: maximum speed 1845 km/h (1,146 mph) at 15240 m (50,000 ft); service ceiling 15240 m (50,000 ft); range 1740 km (1,081 miles)

Weights: empty 6348 kg (13,995 lb); maximum take-off 13170 kg (29,035 lb)

Dimensions: span (excluding missiles) 6.36 m (21 ft 9 in); length 16.66 m (54 ft 8 in); height 4.09 m (13 ft 5 in); wing area 18.22 m² (196.10 sq ft)

Armament: one 20-mm General Electric six-barrelled cannon, wingtip-mounted Sidewinder air-to-air missiles and up to 1814 kg (4,000 lb) of stores

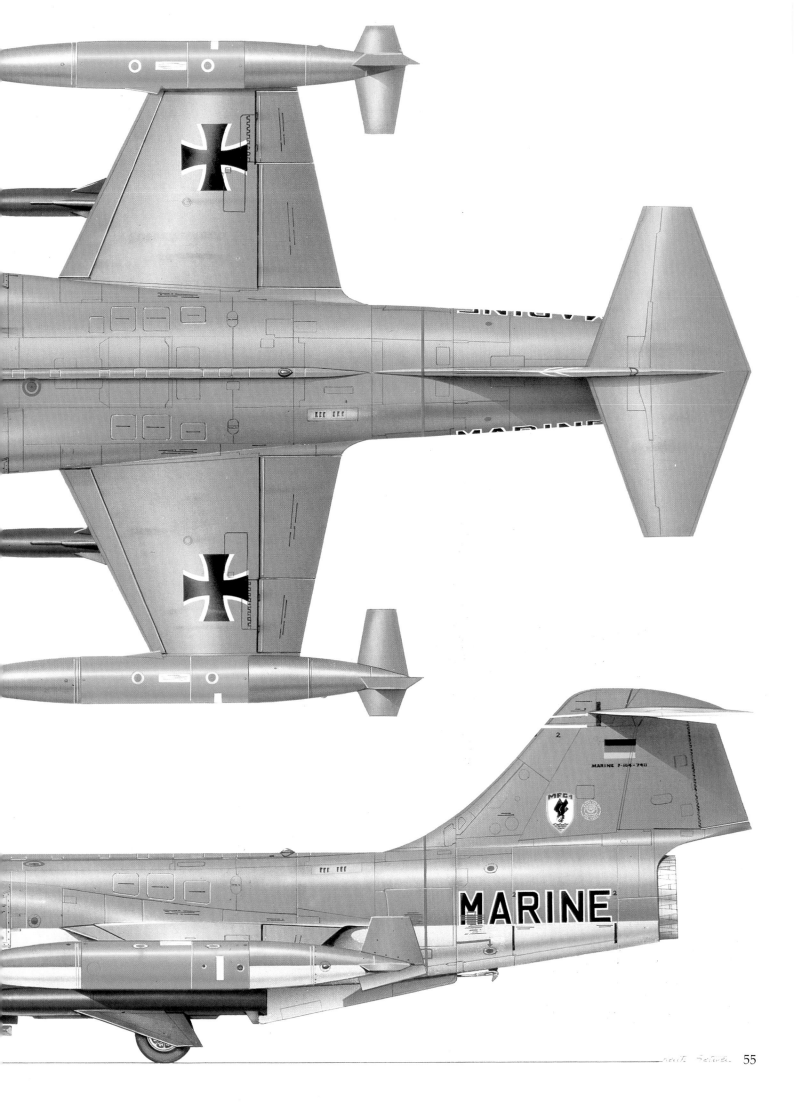

Sukhoi Su-7BMK 'Fitter-A'

In its *Warsaw Pact* days the *Czechoslovakian air force operated large numbers of these early model 'Fitters'. This Su-7BMK 'Fitter-A' displays the features common to all these widely-exported aircraft, such as the bulged nosewheel doors, tail-mounted Sirena radar warning receiver and the additional weapons pylon outboard of the wing fence. Today, however, Czech Su-7s have been largely relegated either to museums or to the scrapheap.*

6430

Specification
Sukhoi Su-7BMK 'Fitter-A'
Type: ground-attack fighter
Powerplant: one 98-kN (22,046-lb) afterburning thrust Lyulka AL-7F-1 turbojet
Performance: maximum speed, clean, 1700 km/h (1,056 mph) or Mach 1.6 at 11000 m (36,090 ft); service ceiling, clean, 15150 m (49,700 ft); typical combat radius 320 km (199 miles)
Weights: empty 8636 kg (19,040 lb); maximum take-off 14800 kg (32,628 lb)
Dimensions: span 8.93 m (29 ft 3¾ in); length 17.37 m (57 ft 0 in); height 4.57 m (15 ft 0 in)
Armament: two 30-mm NR-30 cannon in wing roots, plus underwing pylons for two 750-kg (1653-lb) and two 500-kg (1,102-lb) bombs; limited to weapon load of 1000 kg (2204 lb) when two drop tanks are carried

—Mark Rolfe—

57

North American (Rockwell) RA-5C Vigilante

604

604

604

This **RA-5C** was one of those that began life as an **A-5A** and subsequently underwent complete rebuild in the conversion to the hump-backed reconnaissance aircraft with much greater internal fuel capacity. It did not carry the names of its crew, but everything else is broadcast: Squadron RVAH-14, Modex 604, tail code **AB** of the Atlantic Fleet, embarked aboard CV-67 **USS** John F. Kennedy. RVAH-14 was part of Air Wing **CVW-1,** but after 1972 its place was taken by RVAH-11; and, because of attrition, the squadron's embarked complement was reduced from four aircraft to three.

58

Specification
North American (Rockwell) RA-5C Vigilante

Type: carrierborne reconnaissance aircraft

Powerplant: two General Electric J79-GE-10 turbojets each rated at 8127 kg (17,900 lb) with maximum afterburner

Performance: maximum speed Mach 2.1 (2229 km/h; 1,385 mph) at 12192 m (40,000 ft); cruising limit 2018 km/h (1,254 mph); service ceiling 14750 m (48,400 ft); combat range up to 2414 km (1,500 miles) at 10920-12993 m (35,800-42,600 ft); total internal fuel capacity 13633 litres (3,600 US gal) comprising 2708 litres (715 US gal) in each wing integral tank, 4866 litres (1,285 US gal) in four fuselage tanks and 3315 litres (885 US gal) in three tanks in armament tunnel; provision for four 1515-litre (400-US gal) underwing drop tanks

Weights: empty 17024 kg (37,498 lb); take-off with full internal fuel 29777 kg (65,589 lb); maximum take-off (field or catapult) 36133 kg (79,588 lb)

Dimensions: span 16.17 m (53 ft 0 in); length 23.35 m (76 ft 6 in); height 5.91 m (19 ft 4.75 in); wing area 70.02 m² (753.7 sq ft)

Keith Fretwell.

BAC TSR.2 (XR222)

Specification

Type: two-seat long-range attack and reconnaissance aircraft

Powerplant: two 13885-kg (30,610-lb) thrust Bristol Siddeley Olympus Mk 320 afterburning turbojets

Performance: maximum speed at full load 1352 km/h (840 mph) at sea level, 2185 km/h (1,360 mph, Mach 2.05) at altitude with original engines; standard low-altitude missions, 1,000 nautical miles (1853 km/1,152 miles) radius with 907-kg (2,000-lb) internal bombload, 400 nautical miles (741 km/460 miles) radius with 907-kg (2,000-lb) internal and 2722-kg (6,000-lb) external bombload; ferry range 3,700 nautical miles (6857 km/4,261 miles)

Weights: empty 20344 kg (44,850 lb); maximum 34500 kg (95,900 lb)

Dimensions: span 11.28 m (37 ft 0 in); length 27.13 m (89 ft 0 in); height 7.32 m (24 ft 0 in); wing area 65 m^2 (700 sq ft)

Armament: internal bay for one or two nuclear bombs, six 454-kg (1,000-lb) bombs or long-range tank; four wing pylons for up to 2722-kg (6,000-lb) of bombs, four AS.30 missiles, nuclear bombs, rocket pods or tanks

This three-view shows XR222, the fourth TSR.2, which would have flown in June 1965 had the programme continued. The main landing gear is shown complete with rear damper struts, which were never flown. Note the tabbed 'tailerons', the first to fly as primary roll-control surfaces (except for the air-launched X-15), and the one-piece slab vertical tail. The flaps appear small but were extremely powerful because of the full-span blowing. XR222 managed to survive, because it was taken uncompleted to the Institute of Technology at Cranfield, and later transferred to the IWM at Duxford, where it can be seen today. XR219 was trucked from the apron at Warton to the gunnery range at Shoeburyness, where it is reported to still exist. XR220, already cleared for flight at Boscombe Down, was taken to RAF Henlow and languished there until taken to RAF Cosford, where it is currently exhibited. XR221 and 223 went to Shoeburyness, while 224 to 227 were cut up by oxyacetylene torches.

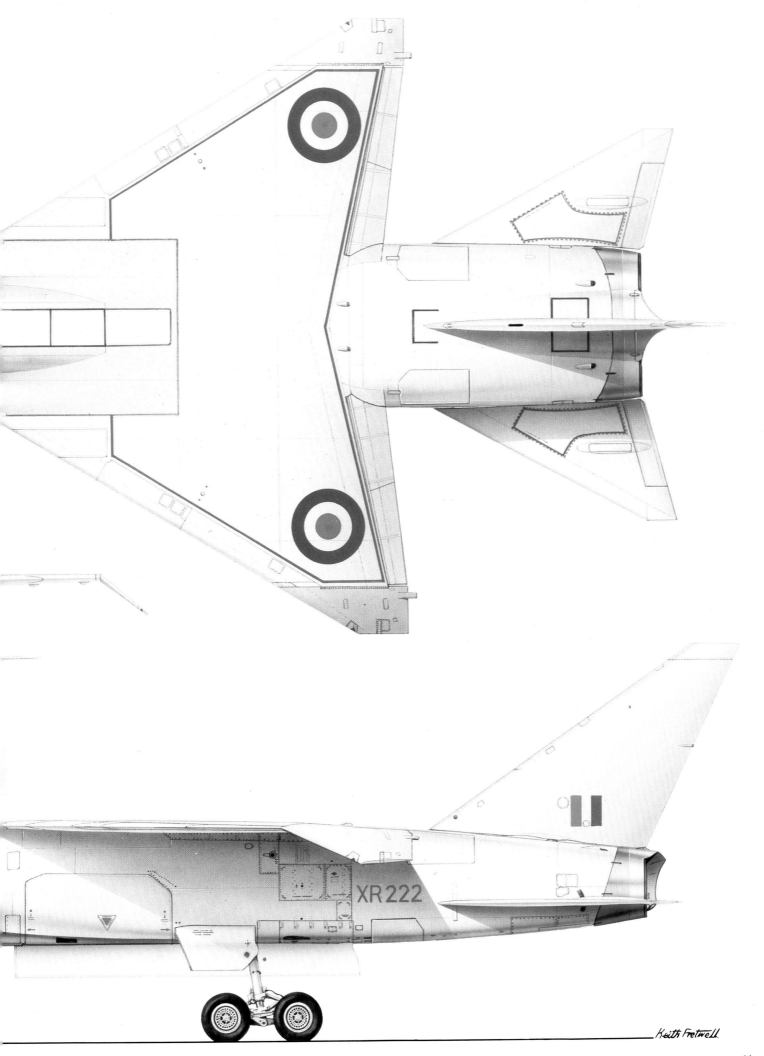

XR222

Keith Fretwell.

Grumman A-6A Intruder

Representing the early generation of Intruders is this A-6A of VA-35 'Black Panthers', armed with a standard load of 18 iron bombs on fuselage and wing MERs (Multiple Ejector Racks). Such aircraft as these brought a new dimension to the war in Southeast Asia, being able to use their sophisticated bombing radar to undertake accurate strikes in weather which other aircraft would have difficulty even flying in. To maximise the precision capabilities of the Intruder, they often flew with other types such as A-4 Skyhawks, providing bomb release commands to the less well-equipped aircraft.

Specification
Grumman A-6A Intruder

Type: two-seat carrier- or shore-based all-weather attack aircraft
Powerplant: two 4218-kg (9,300-lb) thrust Pratt & Whitney J52-P-8B turbojets
Performance: maximum speed 1036 km/h (644 mph) at sea level; cruising speed 763 km/h (474 mph); service ceiling 12,925 m (42,400 ft); range with maximum military load 1627 km (1,011 miles)
Weights: empty 12093 kg (26,660 lb); maximum take-off, catapult 26581 kg (58,600 lb), field 27397 kg (60,400 lb)
Dimensions: span 16.15 m (53 ft 0 in); length 16.69 m (54 ft 9 in); height 4.93 m (16 ft 2 in); wing area 49.13 m² (528.9 sq ft)
Armament: one underfuselage and four underwing attachment points for maximum external load of 8165 kg (18,000 lb)

USS ENTERPRISE
NAVY
VA-35
152940
10
N
G

General Dynamics F-111 'Aardvark'

Specification
General Dynamics F111 'Aardvark'

Type: two-seat multi-purpose attack aircraft

Powerplant: two 11385-kg (25,100-lb) thrust Pratt & Whitney TF-30-P-100 augmented turbofans

Performance: maximum speed at optimum altitude 2655 km/h (1,650 mph) or Mach 2.5; maximum speed at sea level 1473 km/h (915 mph) or Mach 1.2; service ceiling more than 17985 m (59,000 ft); range with maximum internal fuel 4707 km (2,925 miles)

Weights: empty 21398 kg (47,175 lb); maximum take-off 45359 kg (100,000 lb)

Dimensions: span unswept 19.20 m (63 ft 0 in); swept 9.74 m (31 ft 11½ in); length 22.40 m (73 ft 6 in); height 5.22 m (17 ft 1½ in)

Armament: one 20-mm multi-barrelled M61A-1 cannon and one 340-kg (750-lb) B43 bomb, or two B43 bombs in internal weapons bay; three underwing hardpoints on each outer wing panel, the inner four pivoting to keep stores aligned as wings sweep

After its disastrous first combat deployment to South East Asia, the F-111 returned in 1972 and fared considerably better, constantly demonstrating its ability to lay down ordnance with extreme accuracy in all weathers. This aircraft wears the 'NA' tailcode of the 474th Tactical Fighter Wing from Nellis AFB, Nevada, the first recipient of the type in service. It is shown loaded with fin-retarded Mk 82 'Snakeye' bombs and has its weapon bay doors open.

Northrop F-5E

Despite being the first recipient of the second-generation F-5E (illustrated) and F-5F two-seat derivative, the US Air Force only received a few. The initial deliveries were to the 425th TFTS, 58th TTW at Luke AFB, Arizona, where the type was principally involved in training foreign pilots. However, the type's similarity in size and performance to the MiG-21 made it an ideal choice for a dissimilar air combat aircraft to equip the newly-formed Aggressor Squadrons. Most of the USAF's F-5Es therefore wore Soviet-style camouflage and two-digit nose codes. The lion's share of the aggressor force served with the 64th and 65th Aggressor Squadrons of the 57th Fighter Weapons Wing at Nellis AFB, Nevada, although the 527th Aggressor Squadron at RAF Alconbury, England, and the 26th Aggressor Squadron at Clark AB, Philippines, were established to serve the European and Pacific forces, respectively. The F-5 was phased out of this role with the introduction of the F-16, although the Aggressor Squadrons were disbanded as a cost-cutting measure in 1990. Both the US Navy and Marine Corps continue to use the type in their own adversary programmes.

**Specification
Northrop F-5E**
Type: tactical fighter
Powerplant: two 2268-kg (5,000-lb) afterburning thrust General
Electric J85-GE-21 turbojets
Performance: maximum speed Mach 1.64 or 1743 km/h (1,083
mph) at 10975 m (36,000 ft); service ceiling 15790 m (51,800 ft);
maximum range with fuel drop tanks, jettisoned after use 2483 km
(1,543 miles)
Weights: empty 4410 kg (9,723 lb); maximum take-off 11214 kg
(24,722 lb)
Dimensions: span 8.13 m (26 ft 8 in); length 14.45 m (47 ft 4¾ in);
height 4.06 m (13 ft 4 in); wing area 17.28 m² (186 sq ft)
Armament: two 20-mm M-39 cannon in fuselage nose and two AIM-
9 Sidewinder missiles on wingtip launchers, plus up to 3175kg (7,000
lb) of mixed stores

Specification
Mikoyan-Gurevich MiG-25

Type: single-seat interceptor

Powerplant: two Tumanskii R-31 turbojets each with an afterburning thrust of 12250 kg (27,006 lb)

Performance: (estimated) maximum combat speed 2975 km/h (1,849 mph) or Mach 2.8; service ceiling 24395 m (80,000 ft); maximum combat radius 1450 km (901 miles)

Weights: (estimated) empty 20000 kg (44,092 lb); maximum take-off 36200 kg (79,807 lb)

Dimensions: span 13.95 m (45 ft 9¼ in); length 23.82 m (78 ft 1¾ in); height 6.10 m (20 ft 1¼ in); wing area 56.83 m² (611.73 sq ft)

Armament: underwing pylons for the carriage of up to four air-to-air missiles

The subject of this illustration is a MiG-25 interceptor which in early 1975 was serving with an unknown PVO unit in the Soviet Union (not the aircraft in which Lieutenant Belyenko defected in September 1976). It carries the main armament option: four of the giant AAMs known to NATO as AA-6 'Acrid' carried on wing pylons, those on the inboard pylons being fitted with IR homing heads and those on the outer pylons being guided by semi-active radar. A later radar homing head has a receiver aerial of greater diameter inside a bulged white radome, again with a pointed nose.

Keith Fretwell.

69

McDonnell Douglas F-4K Phantom FG.Mk 1

McDonnell Douglas F-4K Phantom FG.Mk 1 of No. 892 Squadron, HMS Ark Royal in 1977. XT872 first flew on 17 June 1968 and, after trials at the Royal Aircraft Establishment at Bedford, the aircraft joined the squadron as '007' in April 1969. The aircraft continued to serve with the squadron until the Phantom was withdrawn from Royal Navy service in September 1978, and was then subsequently transferred to No. 4 Squadron of the Aircraft Engineering Wing at RAF St Athan. No. 892 Sqn's original badge has been replaced by a crowned '77' logo on the nose to mark the Queen's Silver Jubilee.

Specification
McDonnell Douglas F-4K Phantom FG.Mk 1
Type: two-seat multi-role fighter/strike aircraft
Powerplant: two 9305-kg (20,515-lb) afterburning thrust Rolls-Royce Spey RB.168-25 RB 168-25R Mk 202/203 turbofan engines
Performance: maximum speed 2390 km/h (1,485 mph) or Mach 2.25 at 12190 m (40,000 ft); service ceiling 18975 m (62,250 ft); combat radius 958 km (595 miles)
Weights: empty 13397 kg (29,535 lb); maximum take-off 27964 kg (61,651lb)
Dimensions: span 11.71 m (38 ft 5 in); length 19.20 m (63 ft 0 in); height 5.03 m (16 ft 6 in); wing area 49.24 m²
Armament: one 20-mm M61A1 rotary cannon and four AIM-7 Sparrow missiles, semi-recessed beneath the fuselage, or up to 1370 kg (3,020 lb) of weapons on centre pylon, and up to 5888 kg (12,980 lb) on underwing weapons

ROYAL NAVY

ROYAL NAVY
XT 872

04

04

ROYAL NAVY
XT 872

R

Keith I. +

Vought A-7D Corsair II

Specification
Vought A-7D Corsair II

Type: single-seat attack aircraft

Powerplant: one 64.5-kN (14,500-lb) Allison TF41-A-1 (licensed Rolls-Royce Spey) non-after-burning turbojet

Performance: maximum speed, clean 1065 km/h (662 mph) at 610 m (2000 ft) and with 2722 kg (6000 lb) of stores 1041 km/h (647 mph) at 1525 m (5,000 ft); radius of action 885 km (550 miles) with eight 500-lb (227-kg) bombs allowing 30 minutes at low-level in target area, or 1762 km (1,095 miles) with 12 500-lb (227-kg) bombs in hi-lo-hi mission; ferry range 4619 km (2,870 miles) with four 1137-litre (250-Imp gal) tanks

Weights: empty 8973 kg (19,781 lb); maximum take-off 19051 kg (42,000 lb)

Dimensions: span 11.81 m (38 ft 9 in; length 14.06 m (46 ft 1½ in); height 4.90 m (16 ft ¾ in); wing area 34.84 m² (375 sq ft)

Armament: one internal 20-mm M61 Vulcan cannon with 1,000 rounds, plus up to 15,000 lb (6804 kg) of ordnance on six wing and two fuselage pylons

A Vought A-7D Corsair II of the 355th Tactical Fighter Wing, based at Davis-Monthan AFB in Arizona. The aircraft wears the tactical Air Command shield on its fin. Air Combat Command, TAC's successor since 1 June 1992 retains the same emblem, but with the new name. The 355th relinquished their Corsairs for A-10As from July 1976 onwards, and henceforth became known as the 355th Tactical Training Wing. In 1991 the name was changed again to the 355th Fighter Wing, and the Wing assumed responsibility for all A-10 flying at Davis-Monthan, be they its own aircraft, or the OA-10s of the co-located 602nd Air Control Wing. Though its association with the A-7 lasted only from 1971 to 1976, the 355th TFW performed valuable work as the Corsair RTU (Replacement Training Unit) and this aircraft also illustrates the type's considerable punch. A total of 24 low-drag 500-lb Mk 82 bombs are carried on four TERs (Triple Ejector Racks), in addition to the fuel tanks carried on the inner pylons. A pair of AIM-9 Sidewinders are fitted on the 'shoulder' pylons, and the A-7D also has an M61 Vulcan 20-mm cannon.

For much of their career, the SR-71s wore high visibility national markings over the top of the black paint that reduced radar reflectivity. During the last few years of their service all these markings were removed, leaving only a small serial in red on the fin, and the bare essentials in terms of warning stencils. Essentially a simple delta, the SR-71's remarkable shape owed much to the fuselage chines (which were attached to a standard cylindrical fuselage) and the considerable wing/fuselage/nacelle blending. Not only did this have an aerodynamic function, it also helped to reduce radar reflectivity. The sensors, including radars, electronic listening gear and cameras, were housed in four compartments in the chines, or in the detachable nose cone.

Specification
Lockheed SR-71 Blackbird
Type: two-seat reconaissance aircraft
Powerplant: two 14742-kg (32,500-lb) thrust Pratt & Whitney J58 afterburning bleed turbojets
Performance: maximum speed Mach 3 to 3.5 at 24385 m (80,000 ft); maximum sustained cruising speed Mach 3; unrefuelled range 4168 km (2,590 miles)
Weights: estimated maximum take-off 77111 kg (170,000 lb)
Dimensions: span 16.94 m (55 ft 7 in); length 32.74 m (107 ft 5 in); height 5.64 m (18 ft 6 in)

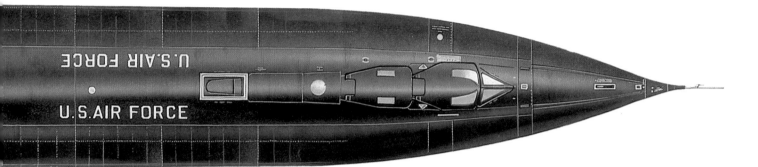

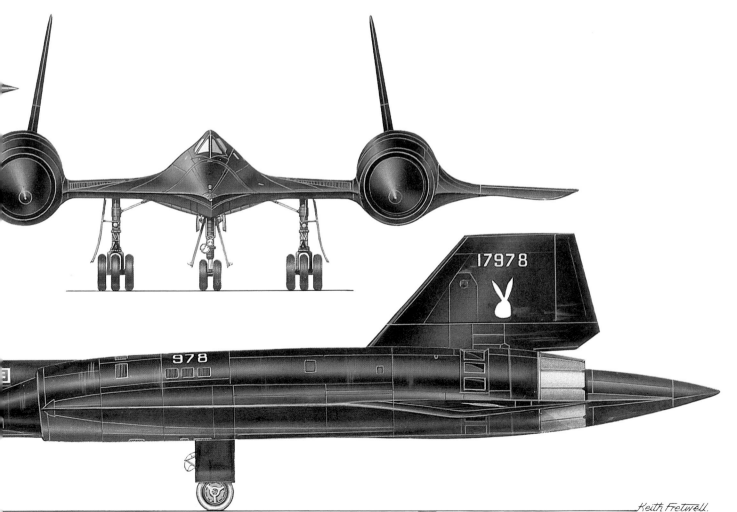

Keith Fretwell.

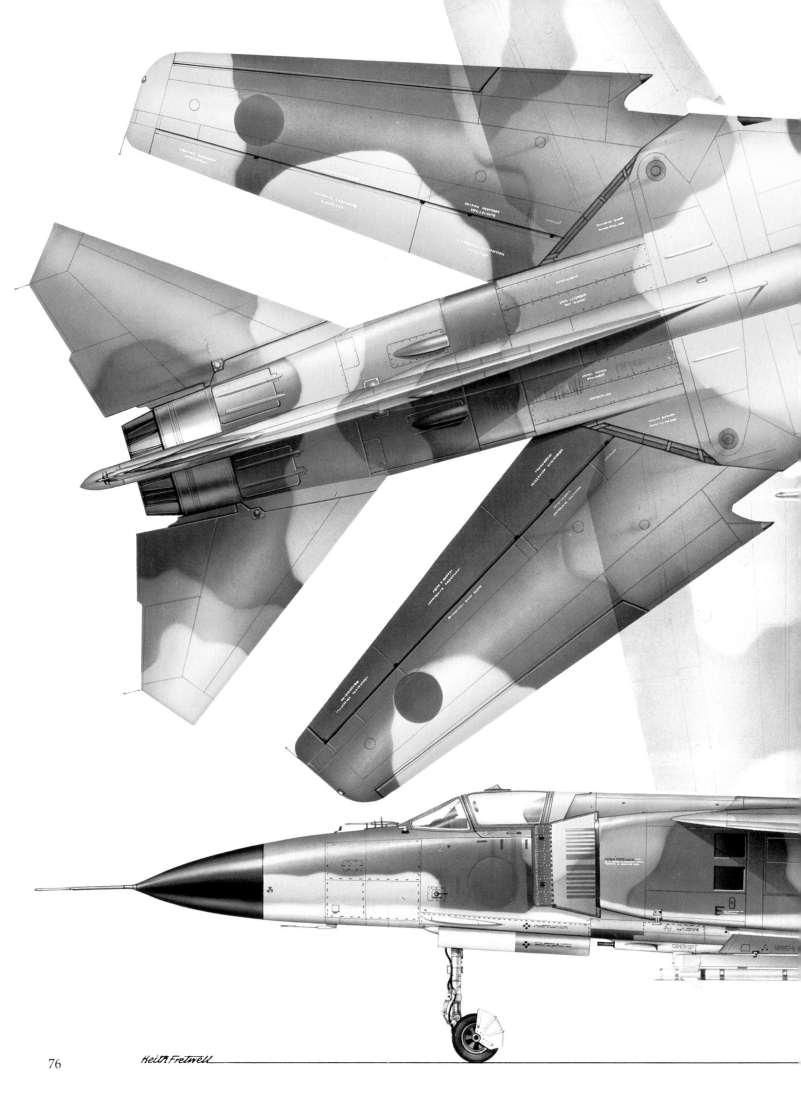

Keith Fretwell

Specification
Mikoyan-Gurevich MiG-23 Flogger-E

Type: single-seat air-combat fighter
Powerplant: one Tumanskii R-29 turbojet engine with afterburning thrust of 12250 kg (27,560 lb)
Performance: (estimated) maximum combat speed 2975 km/h (1,849 mph) or Mach 2.8; service ceiling 24395 m (80,000 ft); maximum combat radius 1450 km (901 miles)
Weights: (estimated) empty 20000 kg (44,092 lb); maximum take-off 36200 kg (79,807 lb)
Dimensions: span 13.95 m (45 ft 9¼ in); length 23.82 m (78 ft 1¾ in); wing area 56.83 m² (611.73 sq ft)
Armament: underwing pylons for the carriage of up to four air-to-air missiles

Selected nations outside the Warsaw Pact have been supplied with MiG-23 fighters by the Soviet Union, Libya being one of the major recipients. This is the downgraded 'Flogger-E' export version, featuring the 'Jay Bird' radar of the MiG-21 in a smaller nose radome, allied to basic AA-2 'Atoll' missiles. Following the January 1989 shoot-down of two

Libyan MiG-23s by US Navy F-14 Tomcats, the US Department of Defense assert that Libya now has AA-7 'Apex' medium-range missile capability for its MiGs. No such missiles were observed by Israeli pilots during the 1982 'turkey-shoot' against Syrian MiG-21s and MiG-23s, when over 80 Arab planes fell to F-15s and F-16s.

SEPECAT Jaguar

Until replaced by *Tornado GR.Mk 1s*, the Jaguar formed the main attack component of *RAF Germany*, flying from the bases at Laarbruch and Brüggen. This aircraft was based at the former, with *No. 20 Squadron*. It carries a typical battlefield air interdiction load, with four Hunting *BL755* cluster bombs under the fuselage and iron bombs under the outer wing pylons. Two 30-mm *ADEN* cannon provides strafing capability. During the war with Iraq, Jaguars from the *RAF*'s surviving squadrons (Nos 6, 41 and 54 Squadrons at *RAF Coltishall*) flew many strikes against targets in *Kuwait* and *Iraq*, using conventional and cluster bombs, and *CRV*7 rockets, the latter particularly effective against coastal targets. For *Gulf* service the Jaguars were hastily modified with overwing pylons for self-defence *Sidewinder* missiles.

78

Specification
SEPECAT Jaguar

Type: single-seat, tactical support aircraft

Powerplant: two Rolls-Royce Turboméca Adour Mk.104 turbofans, each rated at 35.78-kN (8,040-lb) afterburning thrust

Performance: maximum speed Mach 1.6 or 1699 km/h (1,056 mph) at 11000 m (36,090 ft); hi-lo-hi attack radius with external fuel 1408 km (875 miles)

Weights: empty 7000 kg (15,432 lb); maximum take-off 15700 kg (34,612lb)

Dimensions: span 8.69 m (28 ft 6 in); length 16.83 m (55 ft 2½ in); height 4.89 m (16ft 0½in); wing area 24.18m² (260.28 sq ft)

Armament: two 30-mm ADEN cannon, plus up to 4536 kg (10,000 lb) of stores carried on five hardpoints; overwing pylons for air-to-air missiles

NE PAS MARCHER

NE PAS MARCHER

NE PAS MARCHER

NE PAS MARCHER

NE PAS MARCHER

NE PAS MARCHER

12 Escadre de Chasse began receiving the Mirage F1C interceptor in mid-1976, these following the Ouragan, Mystère IVA and Super Mystère B2 successively. The escadre (or wing) has three escadrons (squadrons) equipped with the type, all based at Cambrai-Epinoy. This aircraft is from Escadron de Chasse 1/12, as denoted by its 'Y' codes. Armée de l'Air aircraft often wear different badges on each side of the fin, commemorating World War I squadrons. The hornet badge on the port side of EC 1/12's aircraft is for SPA 89 (a SPAD squadron), while the starboard side carries the tiger's head badge of SPA 162.

12-YN

Specification
Dassault Mirage F1C

Type: single-seat multi-missionfighter/attack aircraft

Powerplant: one 7200 kg (15,873 lb) reheat thrust SNECMA Atar 9K-50 turbojet

Performance: maximum speed at high altitude 2350 km/h (1,460 mph) or Mach 2.2, and at low altitude Mach 1.2; initial climb rate 12780 m (41,930 ft); service ceiling 20000 m (65,615 ft); range with maximum external load 900 km (560 miles)

Weights: empty 7400 kg (16,314 lb); maximum take-off 15200 kg (33,510 lb)

Dimensions: span 8.4 m (27 ft 6¾ in); length 15 m (49 ft 2¼ in); height 4.5 m (14 ft 9 in); wing area 25 m² (269.11 sq ft)

Armament: two 30-mm DEFA cannon, plus a maximum external combat load of 4000 kg (8,818 lb), which can include air-to-air and air-to-surface missiles, air-to-surface rockets, bombs, gun pods and napalm tanks

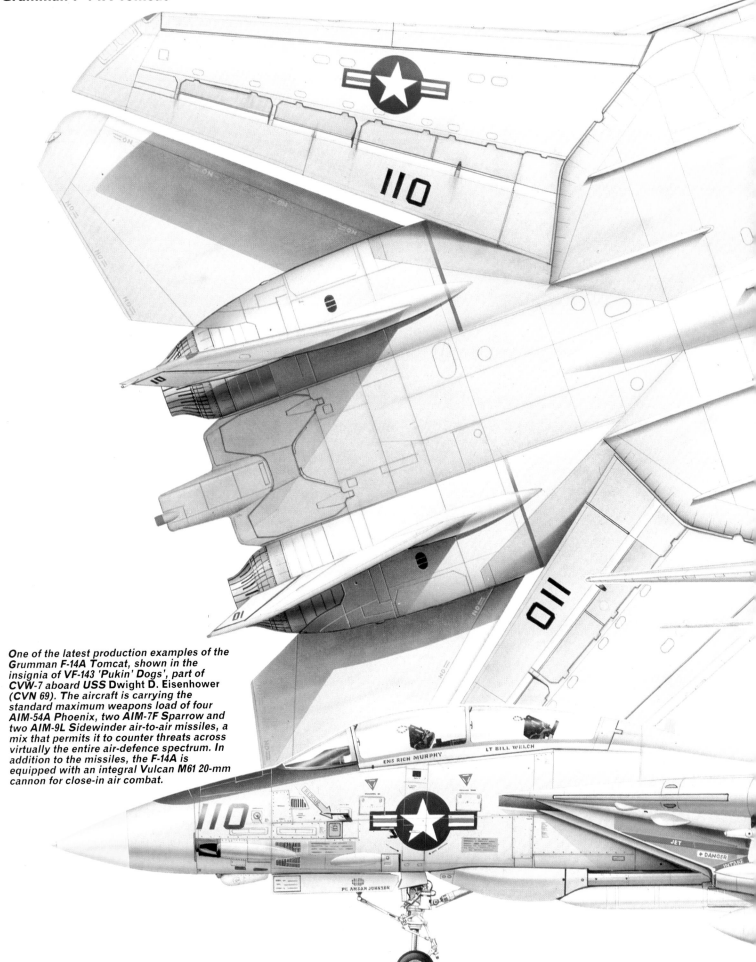

One of the latest production examples of the Grumman F-14A Tomcat, shown in the insignia of VF-143 'Pukin' Dogs', part of CVW-7 aboard USS Dwight D. Eisenhower (CVN 69). The aircraft is carrying the standard maximum weapons load of four AIM-54A Phoenix, two AIM-7F Sparrow and two AIM-9L Sidewinder air-to-air missiles, a mix that permits it to counter threats across virtually the entire air-defence spectrum. In addition to the missiles, the F-14A is equipped with an integral Vulcan M61 20-mm cannon for close-in air combat.

Specification

Type: two-seat shipboard multi-role fighter

Powerplant: two 9480-kg (20,900-lb) thrust Pratt & Whitney TF30-P-412A afterburning turbofans

Performance: maximum speed (clean) 2486 km/h (1,545 mph) or Mach 2.34; time to 18290 m (60,000 ft) 2 minutes 6 seconds; operating radius with four AIM-7F Sparrows 725 km (450 miles)

Weights: empty 18036 kg (39,762 lb); maximum take-off 31945 kg (70,426 lb)

Dimensions: span, unswept 19.55 m (64 ft 1½ in) swept 11.65 m (38 ft 2½ in), overswept 10.15 m (33 ft 3½ in); length 19.10 m (62 ft 8 in); height 4.88 m (16 ft 0 in); wing area 52.49 m^2 (565 sq ft)

Armament: one M61A1 20-mm gun with 676 rounds, plus six AIM-7F Sparrow and four AIM-9 Sidewinder missiles, or six AIM-54A Phoenix and two AIM-9 missiles

Saab Viggen AJ37

Sweden's Flygvapen uses one of the most
sophisticated camouflage patterns in the world,
with three shades of green and one of brown
applied with precision in a curious splinter pattern.
This Viggen is an **AJ37** attack platform, serving
with wing **F7** at **Satenas**, as denoted by the yellow
number on the nose. It is seen equipped for
precision attack with missiles, carrying a pair of
RB75 Maverick missiles on the fuselage pylons and
two of the huge **RB04E** anti-ship missiles under the
wings. The centreline fuel tank is usually carried to
extend range.

Specification
SAAB Viggen AJ37

Type: single-seat fighter
Powerplant: (AJ) RM8A afterburning turbofan, 11800 kg
(26,015 lb) of thrust; (JA) RM8B afterburning turbofan, 12770
kg (28,153 lb) of thrust; fuel 9750 lb
Performance: maximum speed Mach 2 or 2112 km/h
(1320 mph) at 12192 m (40,000 ft); Mach 1.1 or 1335 k/ph
(835 mph) at sea level; initial climb 12200 m (40,000 ft) per
min.; service ceiling: 18300 m (60,000 ft); combat radius
hi-lo-hi 1000 km (620 miles)/ lo-lo-lo 500 km (310 miles)
Weights: empty 11800 kg (26,015 lb); maximum take-off
20450 kg (45,085 lb)
Dimensions: span 10.6 m (34 ft 9 in); length 15.45 m
(50 ft 5 in)
Armament: one fixed belly-mounted 30-mm Oerlikon KCA
cannon, and can carry either four Skyflash semi-active radar
homing (SARH) or four Sidewinder air-to-air missiles

Sukhoi Su-17/20/22 'Fitters'

Late model 'Fitters' are known as *Su-17s* by
Frontal Aviation and as *Su-22s* to their export
customers. All share the bulged spine that
gives the type its distinctive 'humped-back'
appearance, and the taller squared-off tail fin.
'Fitter-H' entered production in the early 1980s
and serves with the Russian and Hungarian
air forces. This aircraft, unlike the subsequent
'Fitter-K', retains the Turmanskii *R-29* engine
of previous models, which is fitted with both
an afterburner and water injection. While
capable of carrying a full range of weapons,
including the *TN-1000* and *1200* series of free-
fall nuclear bombs, the 'Fitter' shown here is
armed simply with a pair of 'Advanced Atoll'
AAMs, a load which does not accurately
reflect its dedicated ground attack role.

Specification
Sukhoi Su-17/20/22 'Fitters'
Type: attack fighter
Powerplant: one 109.8-kN (24,692-lb)
afterburning thrust Lyulka AL-21F-3 turbojet
Performance: maximum speed at
optimum altitude Mach 2.17; service
ceiling 18000 m (59,055 ft); combat radius
(hi-lo-hi) 630 km (391 miles)
Weights: empty 10000 kg (22,046 lb),
maximum take-off 14000 kg (30,865 lb)

Dimensions: span, unswept, 14 m
(45 ft 11¾ in); swept 10.60 m (34 ft 9¾ in);
length 18.75 m (61 ft 6¾ in); height 4.75 m
(15 ft 7 in); wing area, unswept, 40.10 m
(431.65 sq ft)
Armament: two 30-mm cannon in wing
roots, plus eight external pylons for up to
4000 kg (8,818 lb) of mixed stores that can
include air-to-surface missiles such as AS-7
(NATO 'Kerry'), bombs, nuclear weapons
and rockets

Specification
Sukhoi Su-35 (Su-27m)

Type: long-range, twin-engine air-superiority fighter

Powerplant: 2 Lyulka AL-31F afterburning turbofans, 12,500 kg (27,500 lb) of thrust each

Performance: maximum speed Mach 2.35, 2550 k/ph (1,527 mph) at 11000 m (36,000 ft); Mach 1.1, 1520 k/ph (1,527 mph) at sea level; initial climb 15243 m per min. (50,000 ft per min.); service ceiling 18293 m (60,000 ft); combat radius 1553 km (930 miles); maximum range 4000 km (2,580 miles)

Weights: normal loaded 22000 kg (48,400 lb); maximum take-off 30000 kg (66,000 lb)

Dimensions: span 14.7 m (48 ft 2 in); length 21.92 m (71 ft 11 in)

Armament: six wing pylons (including two at the tips) and two fuselage pylons under the engine in-takes, all for air-to-air missiles; standard load is six AA-10, Alamo medium-range radar-guided missiles on the fuselage and underwing pylons, and two AA-8 Aphid or AA-11 Archer short-range infrared-homing missiles on each wingtip; maximum capacity of 6000 kg (13,225 lb) of bombs or air-to-surface missiles

This aircraft is one of six **Su-35 (Su-27M)** prototypes – probably the third, but said to have been the fifth to fly. Both **Su-27M/Su-35s** seen so far have carried 70 series codes, perhaps indicating the **OKB** designation **T-10S-70**. The **Su-35** originated as the **Su-27M** and was designed as a follow-on to the basic **Su-27** with better dog-fighting characteristics, better **BVR** capability and improved multi-role capability. Though it appears similar to the **Su-27** it is in many ways a new type, with new systems and some new structure. The **Su-35** is powered by a pair of **NPO** Saturn (Lyul'ka) **AL-31F** turbofans, and equipped with an improved multi-mode radar. This aircraft is carrying a pair of **R-37s** outboard, four **R-77s** and a trio of the new long-range **AAM-L** anti-**AWACS** weapon. The **Su-35** utilises a completely new quadruplex fly-by-wire system, and the cockpit is fitted with three **CRT** displays.

230498305412G

McDonnell Douglas F-15C Eagle

Project Peace Sun saw the delivery of Saudi Arabia's first F-15s. Sixty-two aircraft – 46 F-15Cs and 16 F-15Ds – were delivered to replace long-serving English Electric Lightning F.Mk. 55s. The first aircraft began to arrive in January 1981 and were operational by August of that year. In 1984 two Iranian F-4Es were shot down over the Persian Gulf, but Saudi Eagles saw no further action until the Iraqi invasion of Kuwait in August 1990. Prior to this, the US authorities had imposed a ceiling of 60 aircraft on the RSAF's F-15 fleet, but in the light of events this limit was rapidly disregarded. Twenty-four F-15C/Ds were taken from the 32nd Tactical Fighter Squadron and 36th Tactical Fighter Wing in Holland and Germany, and used to form the newly-created No. 42 Squadron at Dhahran. Saudi military aircraft use their squadron number to form the first half of their serials, and the rough stencilling of RSAF titles on the nose of this Eagle also marks it out as one of the hastily transferred aircraft. This F-15C is armed with four late-model AIM-9L Sidewinders which were supplied to replace the less-capable AIM-9Ps in stock. A quartet of AIM-7M Sparrows is also carried. A further mix of 12 F-15C/Ds have been ordered and are currently being delivered. In addition a far larger order for attack-capable F-15Fs has just been approved by the US Congress.

Specification
McDonnell Douglas F-15C Eagle
Type: single-seat air-superiority fighter
Powerplant: two 106-kN (23,930-lb) afterburning thrust Pratt & Whitney F100-PW-100 turbofans
Performance: maximum speed (high, clean) Mach 2.5; zoom ceiling 30480 m (100,000 ft); unrefuelled flight endurance 5 hours 15 minutes
Weight: maximum take-off 30844 kg (68,000 lb)
Dimensions: span 13.05 m (42 ft 9¾ in); length 19.43 m (63 ft 9 in); height 5.63 m (18 ft 5½ in); wing area 56.48 m² (608 sq ft)
Armament: one M61A1 20-mm six-barrelled cannon and four AIM-9 Sidewinder, four AIM-7 Sparrow or eight AMRAAM air-to-air missiles; in the secondary attack role up to 7300 kg (16,000 lb) of weapons can be carried externally

القوات الجوية الملكية السعودية
ROYAL SAUDI AIR FORCE

Lockheed S-3A Viking

Specification
Lockheed S-3A Viking

Type: carrier-based patrol/attack aircraft

Powerplant: two 4207-kg (9,275-lb) thrust General Electric TF34-GE-2 turbofans

Performance: maximum cruising speed 686 km/h (426 mph); loiter speed 296 km/h (184 mph); combat range more than 3701 km (2300 miles)

Weights: empty 12088 kg (26,650 lb); normal ASW mission take-off 19278 kg (42,500 lb)

Dimensions: span 20.93 m (68 ft 8 in); length 16.26 m (53 ft 4 in); height 6.93 m (22 ft 9 in); wing area 55.55 m^2 (5980 sq ft)

Armament: weapons including bombs, depth bombs, mines or torpedoes up to 907 kg (2,000 lb) in internal weapons bay, plus cluster bombs, flare-launchers or auxiliary fuel tanks on underwing pylons

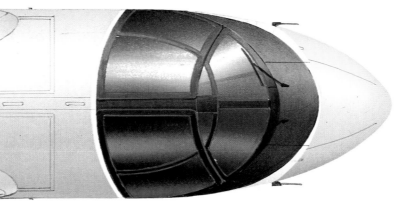

This aircraft represents the early *S-3A* Vikings delivered to the *US N*avy, bearing the highly-coloured markings of *Anti-submarine Squadron 21*, part of *Carrier Air Wing One* aboard *USS* John F. Kennedy. Today the Viking looks considerably different, for most wear variations of the low-visibility grey *Tactical Paint Scheme*. Notable features of the Viking are the podded high bypass ratio turbofans which give sufficient power for some agility and load-carrying, but exceptional endurance. The wing pylons here carry fuel tanks, although weapons can be carried (an *S-3B* was used as a bomber during the Gulf war) or a 'buddy' refuelling pod. In addition to the large nose search radar, the S-3 has passive receivers on the wingtips, and a magnetic anomaly detector retracted into the rear fuselage.

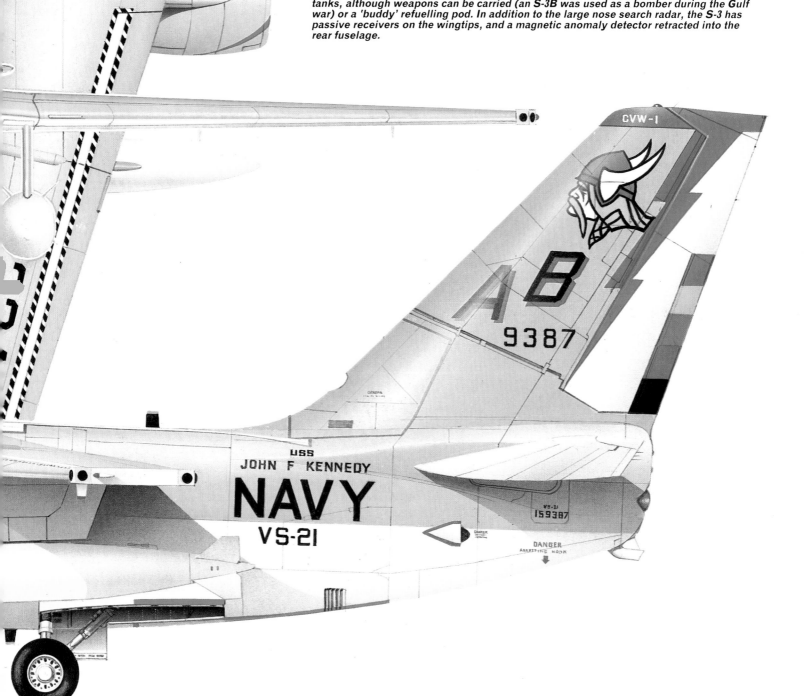

General Dynamics F-16C Fighting Falcon

F-16s form the bulk of USAF assets in Europe, where the type serves with three wings in Germany and one in Spain. All are now of the current F-16C version, identified by the gold-tinted cockpit (said to reduce radar reflectivity) and the additional blade aerial on the lengthened dorsal fillet. Apart from the aircraft of the 52nd TFW at Spangdahlem which are dedicated to the defence suppression mission, European-based F-16s have a dual-role tasking, and are often seen with both air-to-ground and air-to-air weapons. This aircraft is from the 50th TFW at Hahn AB in Germany.

RESCUE

Specification
General Dynamics F-16C Fighting Falcon

Type: single-seat air combat and ground-attack fighter
Powerplant: either one 10800-kg (23,700-lb) Pratt & Whitney F100-PW-220 or one 13150-kg (28,984-lb) General Electric F110-GE-100 afterburning turbofan
Performance: maximum level speed more than 2142 km/h (1,320 mph) or Mach 2.0 at 12190 m (40,000 ft); service ceiling above 15240 m (50,000 ft); operational radius 925 km (575 miles)
Weights: empty 7070 kg (15,586 lb); maximum take-off 16057 kg (35,400 lb)
Dimensions: span 9.45 m (31 ft 0 in); length 15.09 m (49 ft 6 in); height 5.09 m (16 ft 8 in); wing area 27.87m^2 (300 sq ft)
Armament: one General Electric M61A1 20-mm multi-barrelled cannon, a wingtip missile station on each wing plus one underfuselage and six underwing hardpoints enabling the carriage of a 9276-kg (20,450-lb) warload of air-to-air or air-to-surface missiles, ECM, reconaissance or rocket pods, iron or 'smart' bombs or fuel tanks

Keith Fretwell.

95

Dassault Super Etendard

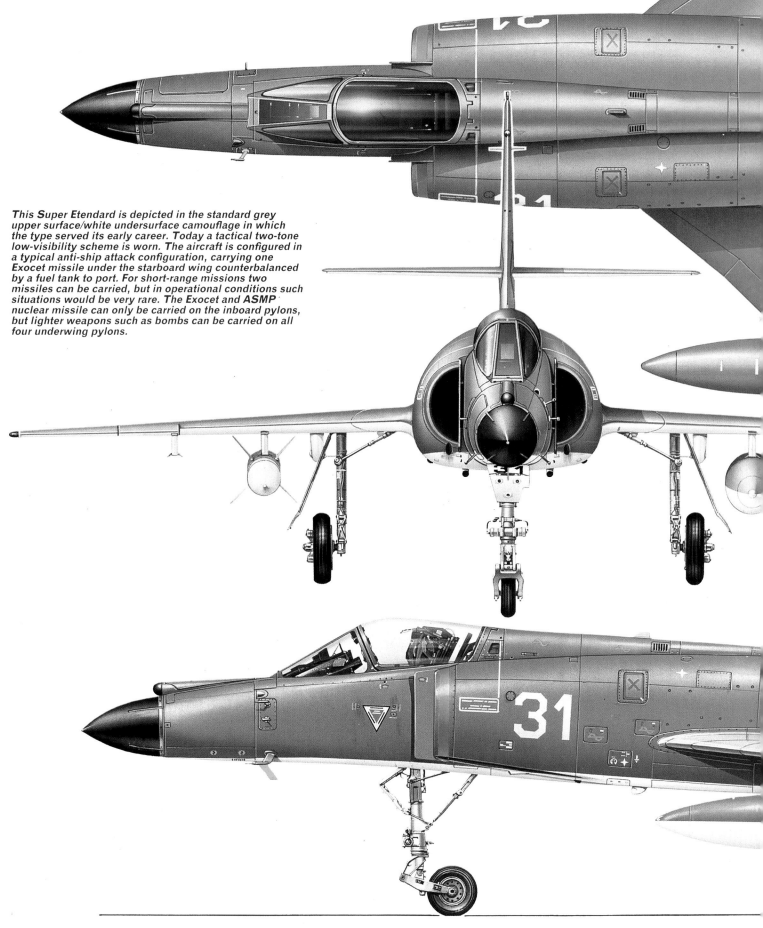

This Super Etendard is depicted in the standard grey upper surface/white undersurface camouflage in which the type served its early career. Today a tactical two-tone low-visibility scheme is worn. The aircraft is configured in a typical anti-ship attack configuration, carrying one Exocet missile under the starboard wing counterbalanced by a fuel tank to port. For short-range missions two missiles can be carried, but in operational conditions such situations would be very rare. The Exocet and ASMP nuclear missile can only be carried on the inboard pylons, but lighter weapons such as bombs can be carried on all four underwing pylons.

Specification
Dassault Super Etendard

Type: carrier-based attack and reconaissance aircraft
Powerplant: one SNECMA Atar 8K-50 5110-kg (11,265-lb) thrust turbojet
Performance: maximum speed at sea level or 1200 k/ph (745 mph); Mach 1 or 1085 k/ph (650 mph) at 10975 m (36,000 ft); initial climb 7500 m (24,600 ft) per min.; service ceiling 13175 m (45,000 ft)
Weights: empty 6500 kg (14,300 lb); maximum take-off 12000 kg (26,455 lb)
Dimensions: span 9.5 m (31 ft 6 in); length 14.31 m (46 ft 11 in)
Armament: typical payloads include one Exocet AM.39 and one drop tank, or one AN.52 free-fall nuclear bomb and one drop tank, or two drop tanks and two Matra R.550 Magic air-to-air missiles, or up to 2100 kg (4630 lb) of free-fall bombs, cluster bombs, laser-guided bombs, Napalm and rocket pods; they are also equipped to launch the ASMP nuclear stand-off missile

Keith Fretwell.

Specification
IAI Kfir-C2

Type: single-seat interceptor, patrol fighter and ground-attack aircraft

Powerplant: one 8119-kg (17,900-lb) afterburning thrust General Electric J79-J1E turbojet

Performance: maximum speed 2445 km/h (1,520 mph) or Mach 2.3 above 11000 m (36,090 ft); service ceiling 17680 m (58,000 ft); combat radius as interceptor 346 km (215 miles)

Weights: empty 7285 kg (16,060 lb); maximum take-off 16200 kg (35,715 lb)

Dimensions: span 8.22 m (26 ft 11½ in); length 15.65 m (51 ft 4¼ in); wing area 34.80 m² (374.60 sq ft)

Armament: one 30-mm cannon, and up to 5775 kg (12,732 lb) of external stores on five underfuselage and four underwing hardpoints

This early Kfir is a -C2, complete with full-size canard foreplanes. Wearing the standard sand/brown/green IDF/AF tactical camouflage, it has large orange/black triangles applied to the wings. These were added to help air defences, both on the ground and in the air, differentiate between Israeli Nesher/ Mirage/Kfir fighters from the Mirages used by neighbouring Arab air forces. Egypt upset the applecart by applying similar triangles to its own Mirages to confuse Israeli defences. The aircraft is depicted in a typical long-range air defence configuration, with a 1300-litre (286-Imp gal) fuel tank under the centreline, and two 500-litre (110-Imp gal) tanks under the wing. The outboard missiles are the indigenously-produced Rafael Shafrir 2 heat-seeker, similar in many respects to the US AIM-9 Sidewinder, which is also carried by the Kfir. Augmenting the missiles are a pair of internal 30-mm DEFA cannon, each provided with 280 rounds.

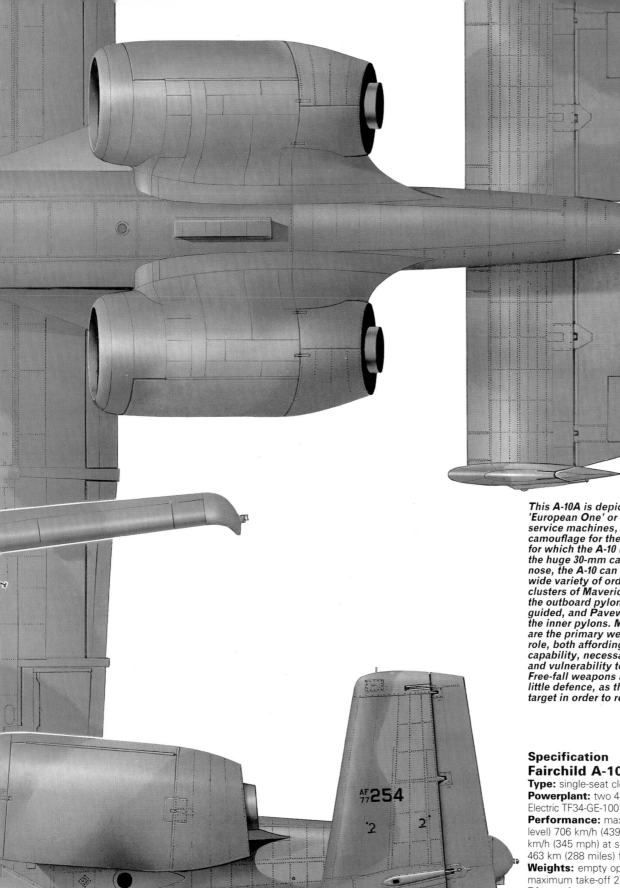

*This A-10A is depicted in the standard 'European One' or 'lizard' scheme adopted for service machines, this affording excellent camouflage for the very low level operations for which the A-10 is renowned. In addition to the huge 30-mm cannon firing through the nose, the A-10 can be equipped to launch a wide variety of ordnance. Depicted here are clusters of Maverick anti-armour missiles on the outboard pylons, with **HOBOS TV**-guided, and Paveway laser-guided bombs on the inner pylons. Mavericks and the cannon are the primary weapons in the anti-armour role, both affording a fair degree of stand-off capability, necessary given the slow speed and vulnerability to gunfire of the aircraft. Free-fall weapons are used only in areas with little defence, as the aircraft has to overfly the target in order to release them.*

Specification
Fairchild A-10A Thunderbolt II
Type: single-seat close-support aircraft
Powerplant: two 4112-kg (9,065-lb) thrust General Electric TF34-GE-100
Performance: maximum speed (clean, at sea level) 706 km/h (439 mph); cruising speed 555 km/h (345 mph) at sea level; loiter endurance at 463 km (288 miles) from base 1 hour 40 minutes
Weights: empty operating 11321 kg (24,959 lb); maximum take-off 22680 kg (50,000 lb)
Dimensions: span 17.53 m (57 ft 6 in); length 16.26 m (53 ft 4 in); height 4.47 m (14 ft 8 in); wing area 47.01 m² (506 sq ft)
Armament: primary weapon is the General Electric GAU-8/A Avenger 30-mm seven-barrel cannon, with a maximum firing rate of 4,200 rounds per minute. Its magazine contains 1,174 armour-piercing rounds, each weighing 0.73 kg (1.6 lb). In addition, three underfuselage and eight underwing stores pylons have a combined external load capacity of 7257 kg (16,000 lb)

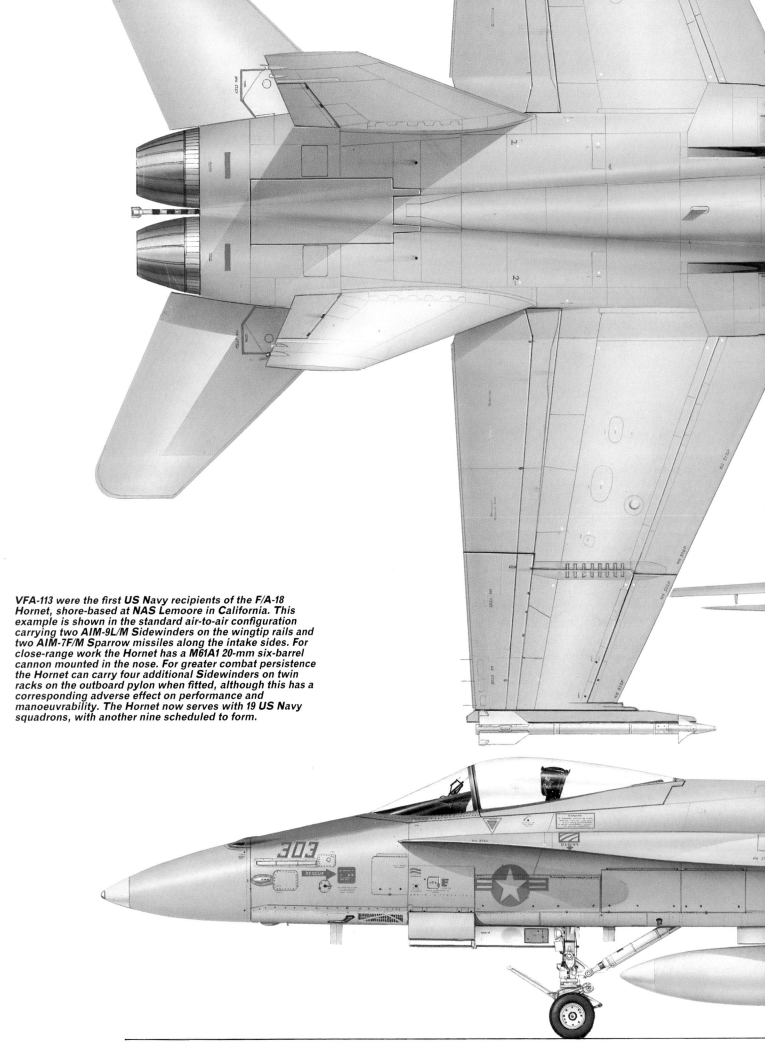

VFA-113 were the first *US* Navy recipients of the *F/A-18* Hornet, shore-based at *NAS* Lemoore in California. *This* example is shown in the standard air-to-air configuration carrying two *AIM-9L/M* Sidewinders on the wingtip rails and two *AIM-7F/M* Sparrow missiles along the intake sides. For close-range work the Hornet has a *M61A1* 20-mm six-barrel cannon mounted in the nose. For greater combat persistence the Hornet can carry four additional Sidewinders on twin racks on the outboard pylon when fitted, although this has a corresponding adverse effect on performance and manoeuvrability. *The* Hornet now serves with *19 US* Navy squadrons, with another nine scheduled to form.

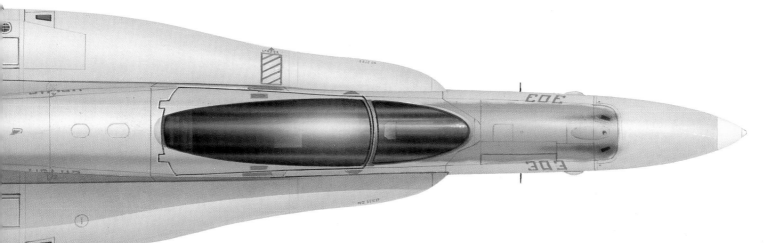

Specification
McDonnell Douglas F/A-18 Hornet
Type: carrier-based naval strike fighter
Powerplant: two 71-kN (16,000-lb) thrust General Electric F404-GE-400 turbofans
Performance: maximum speed (high, clean) Mach 1.8; combat ceiling 15240 m (50,000 ft); combat radius on fighter mission more than 740 km (460 miles)
Weight: maximum take-off for attack mission 22317 kg (49,200 lb)
Dimensions: span 11.43 m (37 ft 6 in); length 17.07 m (56 ft 0 in); height 4.66 m (15 ft 3½ in); wing area 37.16 m² (400 sq ft)
Armament: one M61 20-mm six-barrelled cannon mounted in the nose, plus nine external hardpoints with a maximum capacity of 7700 kg (17,000 lb) of mixed stores, including AIM-7 Sparrow and AIM-9 Sidewinder air-to-air missiles

Keith Fretwell.

Specification
British Aerospace/MBB/Aeritalia Tornado ADV (F2)

Type: two-seat long-range interdiction aircraft (with an interceptor variant)

Powerplant: two 7273-kg (16,000-lb) thrust Turbo-Union RB.199 Mk104 afterburning turbofans; fuel 6982 kg (15,360 lb)

Performance: maximum speed Mach 2.27 or 2505 k/ph (1,500 mph) at 11000 m (36,000 ft); Mach 1.2, or 1536 k/ph (920 mph) at sea level; initial climb 15243 m per min. (50, 000 ft per min.); service ceiling 15243 m (50,000 ft); combat radius, 2.33-hr loiter, 626 km (275 miles)

Weights: normal loaded 21590 kg (47,600 lb); maximum take-off 27986 kg (61,700 lb)

Dimensions: span 13.9 m (45 ft 6 in); length 18.06 m (59 ft 3 in)

Armament: inboard pylons with side-mounted launch rails fortwo AIM-9 Sidewinder air-to-air missiles to be carried at all times; submunitions dispenser for airfield attack: 454-kg (1,000-lb) free-fall and retarded bombs; 454-kg (1,000-lb) Paveway laser-guided bombs; Napalm cannisters; BL.755 cluster bombs; rocket pods, Alarm anti-radiation missiles; Sea Eagle anti-ship missiles; and two tandem pairs of medium-range air-to-air missiles in semi-recessed belly wells

No. 29 Squadron at RAF Coningsby became the first front-line user of the Tornado ADV, becoming operational on 1 November 1987. In the NATO structure it is declared to SACLANT (Supreme Allied Commander Atlantic), and has a maritime air defence commitment. It also has out-of-area taskings, and was consequently one of the units deployed in Operation Granby to Saudi Arabia in 1991. After flying a heavy commitment of combat air patrol missions in support of the Allied effort against Iraq six aircraft returned to Coningsby on 13 March.

BT

ZE203

Iain Wyllie

In Royal Air Force service the Harrier **GR.Mk 5** and its derivatives will adopt the same role as the **GR.Mk 3**s they replace; close air support. For this one of the main weapons at their disposal is the Hunting **BL755** cluster bomb, six of which are carried on this **No. 1 Squadron** aircraft. To utilise the Harrier's excellent agility in the self-defence role, the aircraft also carries a pair of **AIM-9 S**idewinder missiles, these carried on lightweight pylons extending from the outrigger fairings, thus keeping the main pylons free for offensive loads. In addition to the considerable avionics and performance improvements, the large bulged canopy and low sills give the pilot a superb all-round view, a great advantage when operating over the battlefield.

Specification
McDonnell Douglas/British Aerospace
Harrier GR.Mk 5 II

Type: short take-off and vertical landing jet fighter/attack aircraft

Powerplant: Pegasus 105 engine of 95-kN (21,500-lb) thrust

Performance: maximum speed at sea level 1065 km/h (661 mph); maximum speed at altitude Mach 0.92; combat radius with two Harpoons, two Sidewinders and two 1136-litre (250-Imp gal) drop tanks 1128 km (701 miles)

Weights: empty 6344 kg (13, 968 lb); maximum external warload 6003 kg (13,235 lb); maximum take-off 14061 kg (31,000 lb); maximum VTO 9342 kg (20,595 lb)

Dimensions: span 9.25 m (30 ft 4 in); length 14.5 m (47 ft 9 in); height 3.5 m (11 ft 8 in); wing area 21.3 m² (230 sq ft)

Armament: two 25-mm ADEN cannon and nine weapon stations mounted under the fuselage and wings, the extra two wing points for self defence Sidewinder air-to-air missiles, or four Maverick laser-guided air-to-surface missiles, six Mk 83 or 15 Mk 82 bombs, or 12 rocket pods, or four 1136-litre (250-Imp gal) drop tanks

Keith Fretwell

Lockheed F-117 Stealth Fighter

The angular shape of the F-117 is now well-known the world over, yet few have seen the aircraft. Certainly Iraqi gunners had little knowledge of its whereabouts until its bombs exploded, pilots only reporting triple-A fire after the weapons had hit their targets. For the first missions against Iraq, F-117s were escorted by jamming aircraft, but these actually increased the amount of fire before the weapons release, as the jamming gave the Iraqis prior warning of an attack. Afterwards the jammers supporting the F-117s only turned on their equipment after the strike to cover the egress, or used their jammers to deceive defenders. For the most part the F-117s used the GBU-27 bomb, a steel-cased I2000 penetration bomb with the Paveway 3 laser-guidance package. Special treatment makes the GBU-27 'stealthy' so as to preserve the low-observable features of the F-117 during the weapon release. In the light of the Gulf success, the US Air Force was looking at reopening the F-117 line for an additional pair of squadrons. These may be to F-117B standard with bubble canopy and other improvements. A radar in the class of the F-15E's AN/APG-70 may be fitted. If the line does reopen, the Royal Air Force may also show some interest in acquiring the 'Black Jet'.

This 'Black Jet' was flown by Colonel Anthony J. Tolin, commander of the 37th Tactical Fighter Wing. He was previously vice commander and then commander of the 4450th Tactical Group. A long-time F-4 pilot, he also has F-15 and F-16 experience, and flew 95 combat missions in South East Asia, being decorated with the Distinguished Flying Cross, Air Medal with six oak leaf clusters and the Combat Readiness Medal with two oak leaf clusters. Colonel Tolin had three squadrons under his command, the 415th TFS, 416th TFS and 417th TFTS. All three units were formed as night-fighter units in World War II, training initially on Douglas P-70 Havocs before entering action with Bristol Beaufighters.

Specification
Lockheed F-117 Stealth Fighter

Type: single-seat stealth strike fighter
Powerplant: two 4900-kg (10,800-lb) thrust General Electric F404-GE-F102 turbofans
Performance: maximum speed Mach 1; normal operating speed Mach 0.9
Weights: empty operating 13609 kg (30,000 lb); maximum take-off 23814 kg (52,500 lb)
Dimensions: span 13.20 m (43 ft 4 in); length 20.08 m (65 ft 11 in); height 3.78 m (12 ft 5 in); wing area 105.9 m² (1,140 sq ft)
Armament: underfuselage internal weapons can accommodate the full range of USAF tactical fighter ordnance but principally two 907-kg (2,000-lb) bombs of GBU-10/GBU-27 laser-guided type, or AGM-65 Maverick or AGM-89 HARM air-to-surface missiles

Specification
Northrop/McDonnell Douglas
YF-22/23 Advanced Tactical Fighter

Type: single-seat tactical fighter
Powerplant: one aircraft with two 155.7 kN (35,000-lb) thrust Pratt &
Whitney YF119-PW-100 augmented turbofans, and one with similar
thrust General Electric YF120-GE-100 augmented turbofans
Performance: maximum speed Mach 2; supercruise (supersonic
speed without afterburner) Mach 1.6; service ceiling 19812 m (65,000
ft); range on internal fuel 1200 km (750 miles)
Weights: operational empty 16783 kg (37,000 lb); internal fuel 952 kg
(21,000 lb) combat take-off 29,030 kg (64,000 lb)
Dimensions: span 13.2 m (43 ft 7 in); length 20.5 m (67 ft 4 in);
height 4.2 m (13 ft 10 in); wing area 87.8 m² (945 sq ft)
Armament: (planned) one internal long-barrel M61 20-mm cannon,
together with internal bays capable of housing AIM-9 Sidewinders
(eight), AIM-120 AMRAAMS, 'Have Dash 2'

*A remarkable study in how advanced
aeronautical design has become in recent
years is amply provided by the Northrop/
McDonnell Douglas YF-23. Computers with
huge three-dimensional processing capability
have allowed the shape to be crafted for the
optimum combination of low-observability
and operational requirements. The overall
impression of the YF-23 is one of an extremely
stealthy aircraft, with low drag and
consequently exceptionally high cruising
speed, but with a low wing loading for
manoeuvrability.*